MW01623289

LENNON REMEMBERS

The Rolling Stone Interviews

BY JANN WENNER

A Rolling Stone Press Book

FAWCETT POPULAR LIBRARY • NEW YORK

H23769–CBS Fawcett–BX23769

LENNON REMEMBERS

Published by Fawcett Popular Library, a unit of CBS Publications, the Consumer Publishing Division of CBS Inc., by arrangement with Straight Arrow Books

ISBN: 0-445-08191-0

Printed in the United States of America

First Fawcett Popular Library Printing: July 1972

14 13 12 11 10 9 8 7 6 5

I did this interview with John Lennon in early December 1970, at the offices of his business manager, removed by high stories from the daytime traffic in the middle of the music business on Broadway in New York City. We were with Yoko, more or less isolated, in the massive walnut paneled conference room.

Yoko was extremely helpful, adding a word here and there, providing a focus when uncertainties would develop. Because Yoko is a Beatle/John Lennon fan much like the rest of us, she was also unable to resist the laughter that arises from John's compulsive humor, and the awe at some of his statements and ideas; she shares and understands that good old Beatlemania.

Like all events and statements of a particular time, much of this interview has the intuitions and fads of the moment— Dr. Arthur Janov being an obvious example of one of those fads that has subsequently been bitterly denounced.

And I suspect John feels somewhat the same about this interview. Somewhere in here he passes on the warning that he's also just a cat who talks a lot and goes through many changes, leaving much of his prior statements behind him, theories that he's since discarded. Such is the nature of the maturing artist, constantly looking for new avenues and ideas.

The interview was the first time that voluble John poured it all out, or at least the major part of it, after the Beatles broke up. Regardless of his subsequent changes in specific ideas and views, it still holds as *the* statement about the end of the Beatles (because John was the leader of the group) and about John as an artist. It should be approached as history as well as revelation.

A few parts, mainly factual material, were done by cassette-tape on the phone at Christmastime, 1970. I had wanted to add more to the interview, further discussions that would make the reminiscence complete and definitive, but along the way John lost interest. So what we present here is the event as it happened, slightly altered in retrospect and editing.

The interview was given mainly as a personal obligation (and partially as publicity for his about-to-be released solo album), after about two or three years of dealings between myself and John, beginning with printing the *Two Virgins* picture in Rolling Stone, then John's article on the Toronto Peace festival, and a two-hour meeting with Yoko at their house in Ascot when John refused to come downstairs to meet with me because, in Yoko's words, he was 'too paranoid.'

After many phone calls we finally met in June 1970 when he and Yoko came up to San Francisco for a visit during the time they were seeing Janov in Los Angeles. My wife Jane and I spent a weekend with them, showing them a little of San Francisco. The four of us went to see an empty afternoon theater showing of *Let It Be*, the filmic record of the final disinterest/dissolution of the Beatles. After the show—moved at whatever levels, either as participants or deep fans—we somehow cried.

About five months later John and Yoko and I met up in New York to finally record his memories of the Beatles years.

John Lennon is one of the great artists of modern times. There are flaws in the interviews, but here you have it: a remembrance of the most popular entertainers in history.—*Jann Wenner, October 1971.*

LENNON REMEMBERS

Would you take it all back?

If I could be a fuckin' fisherman, I would, you know. If I had the capabilities of being something other than I am, I would. It's no fun being an artist. You know what it's like, writing, it isn't fun, it's torture. I read about Van Gogh, Beethoven, any of them—and I read an article the other day—well, if they'd had psychiatrists we wouldn't have had Gauguin's great pictures. And these fuckin' bastards there just sucking us to death, that's about all that we can do, is do it like circus animals. I resent being an artist, in that respect, I resent performing for fucking idiots who don't know anything. They can't feel; I'm the one that's feeling, because I'm the one expressing. They live vicariously through me and other artists, and we are the ones . . . even with the boxers, when Oscar [Bonneventura] comes in the ring, they're booing the shit out of him. He only hit Clay once and they're all cheering him. That's what I resent, you know. I'd sooner be in the audience, really, but I'm not capable of it. One of my big things is that I wish I was a fisherman. I know it sounds silly, and I'd sooner be rich than poor and all the rest of that shit, but the pain . . . I wish I was . . . ignorance is bliss or something. If you don't know, man, there's no pain, probably there is, but that's how I express it.

What do you think the effect of the Beatles was on the history of Britain?

I don't know about the history. The people who are in control and in power and the class system and the whole bullshit bourgeois scene is exactly the same except that there is a lot of middle-class kids with long hair walking around London in trendy clothes and Kenneth Tynan's making a fortune out of the word 'fuck.' But

First arrival in America

apart from that, nothing happened except that we all dressed up. The same bastards are in control, the same people are runnin' everything, it's exactly the same. They hyped the kids and the generation.

We've grown up a little, all of us, and there has been a change and we are a bit freer and all that, but it's the same game, nothing's really changed. They're doing exactly the same things, selling arms to South Africa, killing blacks on the street, people are living in fucking poverty with rats crawling over them, it's the same. It just makes you puke. And I woke up to that, too. The dream is over. It's just the same only I'm thirty and a lot of people have got long hair, that's all.

Nothing happening except that we grew up; we did our thing just like they were telling us. Most of the so-called 'Now Generation' are getting jobs and all of that. We're a minority, you know, people like us always were, but maybe we are a slightly larger minority because of something or other.

Why do you think the impact of the Beatles was so much bigger in America than it was in England?

For the same reason that American stars are so much bigger in England, I suppose, the grass is greener. And we were really professional by the time we got here: we learned the whole game. When we arrived here we knew how to handle press. The British press are the toughest in the world; we could handle anything. We were all right. I know on the plane over I was thinking, oh, we won't make it, or I said it on a film or something, but that's that side of me. We knew we would wipe 'em out if we could just get a grip on you. So we were new.

Opposite: at the Cavern Club, Liverpool, 1962

And when we got here you were all walkin'

around in fuckin' bermuda shorts with Boston crew cuts and stuff on your teeth, and now they're telling us, they're all saying, 'the Beatles are passé and this is like that, man.' The chicks looked like 1940s horses. There was no conception of dress or any of that jazz. We just thought what an ugly race, what an ugly race. It looked just disgusting and we thought how hip we were. But of course we weren't, it was just the five of us. Us and the Stones were really the hip ones, the rest of England were just the same as they ever were. You tend to get nationalistic, and we used to really laugh at America, except for its music. And it was black music we dug and over here the blacks were laughin' at people like Chuck Berry and the blues singers. The blacks thought it wasn't sharp to dig the really funky black music, and the whites only listened to Jan and Dean and all that.

We felt that we had . . . that the message was listen to this music. It was the same in Liverpool, we felt very exclusive and underground in Liverpool listening to all those old time records. And nobody was listening to any of them except Eric Burdon in Newcastle and Mick Jagger in London. It was that lonely. It was fantastic. We came over here and it was the same: nobody was listening to rock and roll or to black music in America. We were coming to the land of its origin but nobody wanted to know about it.

What was it like to go on tour? I read about cripples coming up to you . . .

Well, that was our version of what was happening. People were sort of touching us when we walked past, that kind of thing, and wherever we went we were supposed to be . . . not like normal. We were supposed to put up with all sorts of shit from Lord Mayors and their wives,

Opposite: The Rolling Stones, 1963

Cripples

and be touched and pawed like *Hard Day's Night* only a million more times. Like at the American Embassy or the British Embassy in Washington or wherever it was, some bloody animal cut Ringo's hair. I walked out of that, swearing at all of them, I just left in the middle of it. But I've forgotten, you tripped me off into that one, what was the question?

The cripples . . .

Wherever we went on tour, like in Britain, or wherever we went, there's always a few seats laid aside for cripples and people in wheelchairs, like that. Because we were famous, we were supposed to have . . . people, sort of epileptics, and whatever they are were in our dressing room all the time . . . we were supposed to be sort of good. You want to be alone and you don't know what to say, because they're usually saying 'I've got your record,' or they can't speak and just want to touch you. And it's always the mother or nurse pushing them on you. They would just say hello and go away but they would push them at you like you were Christ or something, as if there were some aura about you which will rub off on them. It just got to be like that.

We were very sort of callous about it. It was just dreadful. You would open up every night and instead of seeing kids there you would just see a row full of cripples along the front. It was just like that. When we would be running through, people would be lying . . . it seemed that we were just surrounded by cripples and blind people all the time, and when we would go through corridors they would be all touching us. It got like that, it was horrifying.

You must have been still fairly young and naive at that point.

Yeah, well as naive as *In His Own Write.*

Opposite: Eric Burdon and The Animals

MOTHERS

"All the most obnoxious kids"

Surely that must have made you think for a second.

Well, I mean we knew what the game was, the game was the same . . .

It didn't astound you at that point to see you were supposed to be able to—

We were . . . that was a glib way of saying what was going on. It was sort of the in joke that we were supposed to cure them, you know, it was the kind of thing that we would say. Because it was a cruel thing to say. I mean we felt sorry for them, like anybody would, but it was awful and there's a kind of embarrassment when you're surrounded by blind, deaf and crippled people and there is only so much we could say with the pressure on us, to do . . . to perform, and things like that.

It just built up, the bigger that we got, the more unreality we had to face, the more we were expected to do until when you didn't shake hands with a mayor's wife she starts abusing you and screaming and saying 'How dare they!' And there is one of Derek's stories where we were asleep after the session, in the hotel somewhere in America, and the mayor's wife comes and says 'Get them up, I want to meet them,' and Derek said 'I'm not going to wake them up.' She started to scream 'You get them up or I'll tell the press' . . . there was always that, they were always threatening what they would tell the press about us, to make bad publicity about us if we didn't see their bloody daughter and with their braces on their teeth. And it was always the police chief's daughter or the Lord Mayor's daughter, all the most obnoxious kids, because they had the most obnoxious parents. We were forced to see all the time, and we had these people thrust on us. Those were the most humiliating experiences, like sitting with the Governor of the Bahamas when

A Short Essay On Macrobiotics From John Lennon

Asked to write a review of a new magazine of macrobiotic diets, titled Harmony, John Lennon did these drawings. "Greg's" is the health food store in London. The drawings might remind you of a certain well-known album cover.

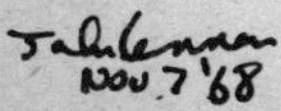

we were making *Help* and being insulted by these junked-up middle-class bitches and bastards who would be commenting on our working-classness and our manners. I couldn't take it, it would hurt me, I would go insane, swearing at them, whatever, I'd always do something. I couldn't take it, it was awful, and all that business was awful. It was a fuckin' humiliation. One has to completely humiliate oneself to be what the Beatles were, and that's what I resent. I mean I did it, I didn't know, I didn't foresee; it just happened bit by bit, gradually, until this complete craziness is surrounding you and you're doing exactly what you don't want to do with people you can't stand, the people you hated when you were ten.

And that's what I'm saying in this album—I remember what it's all about now, you fuckers—fuck you! That's what I'm saying, you don't get me twice.

Are you pleased with your album, your new album [John Lennon/Plastic Ono Band]?

Yes. I'm very pleased. There are lots of things I would have liked to improve.

Like what?

Well, I learned a lot on this album technically. I didn't have to learn so much before because usually there'd be, say, George, Paul and I all listening to it and I wouldn't have to think so much about each individual sound. So there's a few things I learned about bass, where you can get more in and when I lost a track on it; some technical things that irritated me finally.

But as a concept and as a whole thing, I'm pleased.

When you record, do you go for feeling or perfection of the sound?

I like both, but I go for feeling. Most takes are right off and most times I sang it and played it at the same time. I can't stand putting the backing on first then singing, which is what we used to do a lot in the old days. But . . . but they're always dead, you know. They'd gotten to that sort of dead Beatles sound, or dead recording sound. So I like to—some of them are the second take—get them right off.

"Mother"

Your new album starts off with bells. Why?

Well, I was watching TV as usual in California and there was this old horror movie on and I just heard . . . the bells sounded like that to me. They were probably different because those were actually other bells slowed down that I used on the album. They just sounded like that and I just thought that's how to start "Mother." And I knew "Mother" was going to be the first track, so . . .

You said that you wrote most of the songs in California?

Well, a lot of it. Actually I wrote "Mother" in England, didn't I. And "Isolation" in England and a few more. It just seems as though it was all written . . . I finished them off in California. You can go into detail, you will have to push me if you want more detail 'cause otherwise I'll just forget. "Look At Me" was written around the Beatles' double album time; I just never got it done. There are a few like that lying around.

You said that this would be the first Primal album.

When did I say that?

In California.

Yes, well . . . I don't know.

Have you gone off that?

No, no, I haven't gone off, it's just like Primal is like another mirror.

Yoko: He is like any artist, I suppose; he really wants to be honest with himself and the album, and what he does, instead of just patching up something that is sort of interesting or so-so, he really puts himself in it, his life in it. Like when he went to India, he was influenced by the Maharishi . . .

JOHN: Writers take themselves to Singapore to get the atmosphere. So wherever I am, in that way it's a Primal album. But is George's the first Gita album? It's that relevant.

YOKO: The Primal Scream is a mirror, and he was looking at the mirror.

Let's talk about Janov for a second. When you came out to San Francisco you wanted to do an advertisement for him. You wanted to say 'This Is It.'

I think that's something people go through at the beginning of that therapy because you are so astounded with what you find out about yourself that you think, well, surely nobody's heard, surely this is something. Because it happens to you, you think this must be the first time it's happened. So it's full of that. Also we wanted to come out. I need to have a reason for going somewhere otherwise I'm too nervous. So I calmed myself and that was a good way of coming to San Francisco to see you. Then I have an objective; I'm going to do an advert and so we come and I'm going to do this and all that and we sit, settle down and we just talk.

So it is really like that. But I still think the therapy is great, but I just don't want to make it into a big Maharishi thing. You were right to tell me to forget the advert and that's why I don't even want to talk too much about it. If people know what I've been through there and if they want to find out they can find out. Otherwise it turns into *that* again.

So you no longer feel that this is the single thing to do—just one of a number of therapies?

Opposite: Dr. Arthur Janov

I don't think anything else would work on me

Recording without George or Paul

so well. But then of course, I'm not through with it. It's a process that is going on. We primal almost daily and the only difference . . . I don't really want to get this big primal thing going because it gets so embarrassing. The thing in a nutshell: Primal Therapy allowed us to feel feelings continually and those feelings usually make you cry. That's all. Because before I wasn't feeling things. I was blocking the feelings. When the feelings come through, you cry. It's as simple as that, really.

Do you think the experience of therapy helped you become a better singer?

Maybe.

Do you think your singing is better on this album?

It's probably better because I had the whole time to myself. I mean I'm pretty good at home with me tapes. This time it was my album and I didn't have to . . . it used to get a bit embarrassing in front of George and Paul because we know each other so well . . . oh he's trying to be Elvis, oh he's doin' this now. We were a bit super-critical of each other so we inhibited each other a lot. And now I have Yoko there, and Phil there, alternatively and together, who sort of love me, so I can perform better; and I relaxed, you know. I've got a studio at home now and I think it'll be better next time because that's even less inhibiting than going to EMI. It's like that. But the looseness of the singing was developing on "Cold Turkey" from the experience of Yoko's singing. You see she does not inhibit her throat.

It says on the album that Yoko does wind.

Yes, well, she plays wind, she played the atmosphere.

Yoko: I was around, that's all.

John: She has a musical ear and she can produce rock and roll. She can produce me, which she did for some of the tracks. I'm not going to start saying that she did this and he did that, but when Phil couldn't come at first . . . you don't have to be born and bred in rock; she knows when a bass sounds right and when a guy is playing out of rhythm and when the engineer . . . she has a bit of trouble, the engineer thinks 'well, who the hell is this?' 'What does she know about it?' So, she did that for me.

"The Working Class Hero"

"Working Class Hero" sounds like an early Dylan song.

Anybody that sings with a guitar and sings about something heavy would tend to sound like Dylan. I'm bound to be influenced by those because that is the only kind of real folk music I ever listen to. I never liked the fruity Judy Collins and Baez and all of that stuff. So the only folk music I know is stuff about miners up in Newcastle, or Dylan. So in that way I've been influenced, but it doesn't sound like Dylan to me. Does it sound like Dylan to you?

Only in the instrumentation.

That's the only way to play. I never listen that hard to him, you know.

What is November 5th?

In England it's the day they blew up the Houses of Parliament. We celebrate it by having bonfires every November the 5th. It just was an ad lib; it was about the third take and I got to the 'remember' and it begins to sound like Frankie Laine, you know when you sing (sings) "Remember . . . remember the fifth of November." And I just broke up and it went on for about another seven or eight minutes. It was just ad libbing and goofing about. But then I cut it there and just exploded 'cause it was a good joke. Haven't you ever heard of Guy Fawkes? That's

"God is a concept by which we measure our pain."

Guy Fawkes Day and I thought it was poignant that we should blow up the Houses of Parliament.

Do you get embarrassed sometimes when you hear the album, when you think about how personal it is?

No. Sometimes I can hear it and be embarrassed just by the performance of either the music or by the statements and sometimes I don't. I change daily, you know. Just before it's coming out I can't bear to hear it in the house or play it anywhere, but a few months before that I can play it every hour. It just changes all the time, you see. Sometimes I used to listen to something—Buddy Holly or anything—and one day the record will sound twice as fast as the next day. Did you ever experience that on a single? I used to have that, like "Hound Dog." One day it would sound very slow and one day it would sound very fast. It was just my feeling towards it . . . the way I heard it. That's where you have to make the artistic judgment to say this is the take and this isn't. That's where you have to make the decision when it sounds reasonable.

What is your concept of pain?

Pain is the pain we go through all the time. You're born in pain. Pain is what we're in most of the time. And I think the bigger the pain, the more gods we need.

There is a tremendous body of literature, of philosophical literature, about god as a measurement of pain.

I never heard about it. You see it was my own revelation. I don't know who wrote about it, or what anybody else said, I just know that's what *I know.*

Yoko: But you just felt it.

John: Yes I felt it. When I felt it, it's like I was crucified. So I know what they're talking about now.

George Martin
Phil Spector

What is the difference between George Martin and Phil Spector?

George Martin . . . I don't know. You see for quite a few of our albums—like the Beatles' double album, George Martin didn't really produce it. I don't know whether this is scandalous, but he didn't. In the early days I can remember what George Martin did.

What did he do?

In the early days he would translate . . . if Paul wanted to use violins, he would translate it for him. Like "In My Life," there's an Elizabethan piano solo in it. He would do things like that. We would say 'play like Bach or something' or 'could you put twelve bars in there?' And he helped us develop a language to talk to musicians.

Because I'm very shy, and many, many reasons, I didn't very much go for musicians. I didn't like to have to go and see twenty guys sitting there and try to tell 'em what to do because they're always so lousy anyway. So apart from the early days, when I did it myself, I didn't have much to do with it.

Why did you use Phil now instead of George?

Well it's not instead of George Martin. I would not use anybody rather than use George Martin. That's nothing personal against George Martin, he just doesn't . . . he's more Paul's style of music than mine. It's a drag to do both, to go in the recording studio and then you gotta run back and say 'Did you get it?'

Did Phil make any special contribution?

Yes, yes. Phil, I believe, is a great artist and like all great artists he's very neurotic. But we'd done quite a few tracks together, Yoko and I, and she'd be encouraging me in the other room and all that, and . . . at one point in the middle

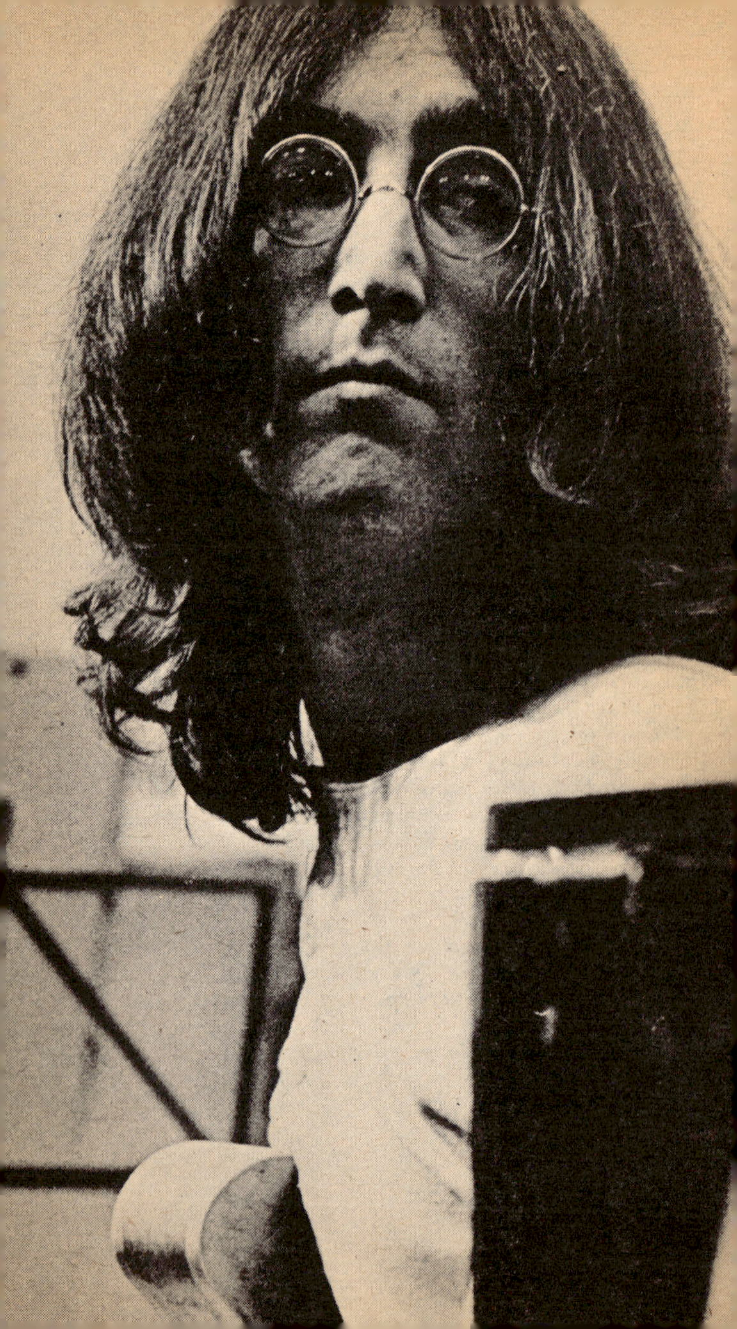

we were just lagging and Phil moved in and brought in a new life because we were getting heavy and we had done a few things and the thrill of recording had worn off a little. You can hear Spector here and there . . . there are no specifics, you can just hear him.

Writing 'first person music'

Let me ask again: are you pleased with the new album?

I think it's the best thing I've ever done. I think it's realistic and it's true to me that has been developing over the years from "In My Life," "I'm a Loser," "Help," "Strawberry Fields." They're all personal records. I always wrote about me when I could. I didn't really enjoy writing third person songs about people who lived in concrete flats and things like that. I like first person music. But because of my hangups, and many other things, I would only now and then specifically write about me. Now I wrote all about me and that's why I like it. It's me! And nobody else. So I like it.

There is a thing . . . basically the honesty of it.

Just it's real. It's about me and I don't know about anything else, really. The only true songs I ever wrote were "Help" and "Strawberry Fields." I can name a few . . . I can't think of them offhand, that I always considered my best songs. They were the ones I really wrote from experience and not projecting myself into a situation and writing a nice story about it which I always found phoney . . . I'd find occasion to do it because I'd have to produce so much work or because I'd be so hung up I couldn't even think about myself.

For instance, on this album there is practically no imagery at all.

No, because there was none in my head. There were no hallucinations.

Constructing a litany

There were no 'newspaper taxis.

Then I was consciously writing poetry, and that's self-conscious poetry. Actually that's Paul's line. But the poetry on this album is superior to anything I've done because it's not self-conscious in that way. I had least trouble writing the songs of all time.

YOKO: There's no bullshit.

The music is very simple and very sparse.

Well I always liked simple rock. There's a great one in England now, "I Hear You Knocking." I liked "Spirit in the Sky" a few months back. I always liked simple rock and nothing else. And I was influenced by acid and got psychedelic, like the whole generation, but really, I like rock and roll and I express myself best in rock. I had a few ideas to do this with "Mother" and that with "Mother," but when you just listen, the piano does it all for you, your mind can do the rest of it. I think the backings on mine are as complicated as the backings on any record you've ever heard; if you've got an ear, you can hear. Anybody knows, any musician will tell you, just play a note on a piano, it's got all the harmonics in it. So it got to that. I didn't need anything else.

How did you put together that litany in "God"?

What's litany?

"I don't believe in magic," that series of statements.

Well, like a lot of the words, they just came out of me mouth. It started off like that, you know . . . "God" was stuck together from three songs almost. I had the idea "God is the concept by which we measure pain," so when you have a word like that you just sit down and sing the first tune that comes into your head and the tune is simple 'cause I like that kind of music and then I just rolled into it . . . (sings) "I don't believe in magic" . . . and it was just going on in my head and I Ching and Bible and the first three or four just came out, whatever came out, you know.

"The dream is over"

When did you know that you were going to be working towards "I don't believe in Beatles"?

I don't know when I realized I was putting down all these things I didn't believe in. I could have gone on, it was like a Christmas card list. I thought 'Where do I end?' Churchill . . . and who have I missed out . . . it got like that, you know, and I thought I had to stop.

Yoko: He was going to have a do-it-yourself, too.

John: Yeah, I was going to leave a gap and say just fill in your own, you know, and put whoever you don't believe in. It had just got out of hand. But Beatles was the final thing because it's like I no longer believe in myth, and Beatles is another myth. I don't believe in it, the dream is over. And I'm not just talking about the Beatles, I'm talking about the generation thing. The dream is over. It's over and we gotta—well I have anyway, personally—get down to so-called reality.

When did you become aware that that song was to be the one that is being played the most?

Well, I didn't know that because up here they're playing . . . I don't know, I'll be able to tell in a week or so really what's going on, 'cause they started off playing "Look At Me" because it was easy and they probably thought it was the Beatles or something. "God" and "Working Class Hero" are probably the best, whatevers, you know . . . sorts of ideas, or feelings on the record.

Why did you choose to refer to Dylan as Zimmerman and not as Dylan?

'Dylan' vs 'Zimmerman'

Because Dylan is bullshit, Zimmerman is his name.

Yoko: He changed his name.

John: You see I don't believe in Dylan. I don't believe in Tom Jones either in that way. Zimmerman is his name. My name isn't John Beatle, it's John Lennon. You know, just like that.

Why did you tag "Mummy's Dead" at the end?

Because that's what's happened. All these songs just came out of me. I didn't sit down to think 'I'm going to write about my mother,' or I didn't sit down to think 'I'm going to write about this, that or the other.' They all came out, like all the best work anybody ever does, whether it's an article or what, it's just the best ones that come out. And all these came out because I had the time—and when you do, if you are on holiday or in therapy, wherever you are, if you'd spend time . . . like in India I wrote the last batch of best songs. I could write a lot like "I'm So Tired" and "Yer Blues," where they were pretty realistic. They were about me and they always struck me as—what's the word?—funny, ironic, or something, that I was writing supposedly in the presence of guru and meditating so many hours a day, I was writing "I'm So Tired" and songs of such pain as "Yer Blues." Which I meant. It wasn't just me, I was trying to express it in blues idiom.

Yoko: "Cold Turkey," too.

John: "Cold Turkey." I was right in the Maharishi's camp writing "I wanna die."

Was "Yer Blues" also deliberately meant to be a parody of the English blues scene?

Well, a bit, because I'm a bit . . . we all were self-conscious, and Beatles were super self-conscious people, about parodying Americans, which

"Yer Blues" and the bullshit movement

we do and nave done. I know we developed our own style, but we still in a way parody American music. This is interesting: in the early days in England all the groups were like Elvis and a backing group. And the Beatles deliberately didn't move like Elvis, that was our policy, because we found it stupid and bullshit. And then Mick Jagger came out and resurrected bullshit movement, you know, wiggling your arse and that. So then people began to say, 'Well, the Beatles are passé because they don't move.' But we did it as a conscious thing.

When we were younger we used to move, we used to jump around and do all the things they're doing now like going on stage with toilet seats and shitting and pissing. That's what we were doing in Hamburg, and smashing things up. It wasn't a thing that Pete Townshend sort of worked out, it is something that you do when you play six or seven hours. There is nothing else to do, you smash the place up and you insult everybody. But we were groomed and we dropped all of that and the same with . . . whatever it was we started off talking about, which was what, about singing, what was it? What was the beginning of that?

Was "Yer Blues" deliberately parodying—

Yeah, yeah. So there's a self-consciousness about suddenly singing blues. I mean we were all listening to Sleepy John Estes and all that in art school, like everybody else. But to sing it was something else. And so I'm self-conscious about doing it. I think Dylan does it a lot you know. In case he's not sure of himself he makes it double entendre. So therefore he is secure in his hipness. But George was saying don't . . . or Paul was saying 'Don't call it "Yer Blues" just say it straight.' But I was self-conscious and I

Opposite: Sleepy John Estes

Yoko (singing)

went for "Yer Blues." I think all that has passed now because I think musicians . . . we've all got over it, that self-consciousness.

Yoko: You know I think John, being John, is a bit unfair to his music in a way. I'd like to just add a few things. He can go on for an hour or something . . . One thing is about Art Janov. Say if John fell in love, you know he is always falling in love with all sorts of things, from the Maharishi to what not . . .

John: Nobody knows there is a point on the first song on Yoko's track where the guitar comes in, and even Yoko thought it was her voice, because we did all Yoko's in one night, the whole session. It was just fantastic.

The whole album?

Yeah, except for Ornette. There's a track with Ornette Coleman that was from the past that we put on to show people that she wasn't discovered by the Beatles and that she's been around a few years. We got stuff of her with Cage, Ornette Coleman . . . We are going to put "Oldies But Goldies" out next for Yoko.

Yoko: I was just saying that he just goes on falling in love with all sorts of things, but it is like, say, if he fell in love with some girl, or something and he wrote this song. Who he fell in love with is not very important. It's the outcome of it, you know, the song itself is important.

For instance, you have to say that a song like "Well, Well, Well" is connected with Primal Therapy, or the theory of Primal Therapy.

Why?

The screaming.

No. No, but listen to "Cold Turkey."

Yoko: He's screaming already there.

John: Listen to "Twist and Shout." I couldn't sing the damn thing, I was just screaming. Listen to it . . . "Wop bop a loo, wop a wop bop loo" . . . Don't get the therapy confused with the music.

Screaming (music vs. therapy)

Yoko: I was screaming . . .

John: Yoko's whole thing was that scream. Listen to "Don't Worry Kyoko." It's one of the fuckin' best rock and roll records ever made. Listen to it and play "Tutti Frutti." Listen to "Don't Worry Kyoko" on the other side of "Cold Turkey." You see, I'm digressing from mine, but if somebody with a rock oriented mind can possibly listen to her stuff you'll see what she's doing. It's fantastic. It's as important as anything we ever did and as important as anything the Stones or Townshend ever did. Listen to it and you'll hear what she is putting down. On "Cold Turkey" I'm getting towards it. I'm influenced by her music 1000 percent more than I ever was by Dylan. She makes music like you've never heard on earth. And when the musicians play with her they're inspired out of their skulls. I don't know how much they play it later . . . we've got a cut of her from the Lyceum in London, 15 or 20 musicians playing with her from Bonnie and Delanie and the fucking lot, and we played the tracks the other night. It's the most fantastic music I've ever heard. And they've probably gone away and forgotten all about it. It's fantastic. It's like 20 years ahead of its time.

Anyway, back to mine. Listen to "Cold Turkey."

When you were talking about "Cold Turkey" you said 'That's not a song, that's a diary.'

Yeah, well, so is this.

Yoko: Everything is.

John: So is this, you know. I announced "Cold Turkey" at the Lyceum saying 'I'm going to sing a song about pain.' So pain and screaming

Heroin

was before Janov. I mean Janov showed more of my own pain . . . I mean I went through therapy, like I told you, with him and I'm probably looser all over.

Are you less paranoid now?

No, but I can feel my own fear. I can feel my own pain therefore I can handle it better than I could before, that's all. I'm the same only there's a channel, it doesn't just remain in me, it goes around. I can move a little easier.

What was your experience with heroin?

Heroin? It was just not too much fun. I never injected it or anything. We sniffed a little when we were in real pain. I mean we just couldn't . . . people were giving us such a hard time.

Yoko: We didn't get into it so much.

John: We got such a hard time from everyone. And I've had so much shit thrown at me and at Yoko, especially at Yoko. People just . . . like Peter Brown in our office, and you can put this in, after we come home from six months he comes down and shakes my hand and doesn't even say hello to her. And that's going on all the time. We were getting so much pain that we have to do something about it. And that's what happened to us, you know. We took "H" because of what the Beatles and their pals were doing to us. But we got out of it.

Yoko: Let's go back to the album . . . You know, like he was saying about Phil Spector—

John: I mean they didn't set down to do it, but people's things came out at that period, you know, and I don't forget.

Yoko: You know he really produced his own stuff. Phil is, as you know, well known as a very skillful sort of technician in electronics and engineering . . .

Opposite: Phil Spector

John: But let's not take away from what he

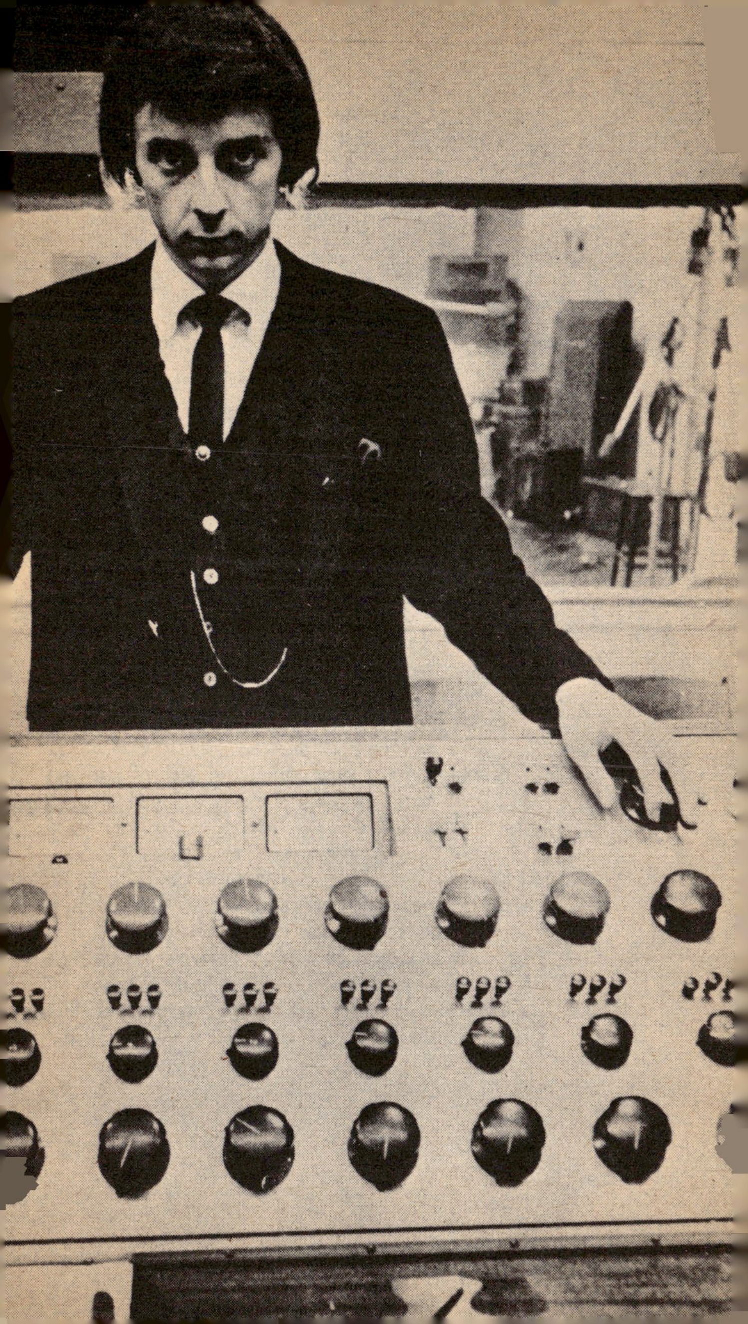

did do, which was bring a lot of energy and taught me a lot and I would use him again.

Yoko: Yes, but he is so definite about things . . .

John: But I know what I want. But Phil is more . . . When I say to Phil I want this, he gets it for me.

Yoko: It's not a Spector sound, in other words.

John: No, no, you can hear Spector on the album, and you can hear—

You can hear the voice the way Spector—

No, no, that was me. I did that before Phil came.

Yoko: Right, exactly.

John: Right, I did quite a lot of it before Phil came.

Yoko: Also that "Mother" bell . . . You were saying that it was a church bell and it is connected with his childhood. And he was always saying 'Sundays I heard church bells.'

John: I read an article on some new Southern country singer who wrote something like Sunday is a lonely day. It's that feeling, too.

In past records it's always . . . well in Sgt. Pepper *it's 'come see the show,' and this record is so personal.*

You see, Paul said come and see the show, I didn't. I said "I read the news today, oh boy," that's what I said, and "Mr. Kite," mind you.

You're "Mr. Kite"?

No, no, I wrote that as a pure poetic job. To write a song, sitting there . . . and I wanted, had to write because it was time to write and I had to write it quick because otherwise I wouldn't have been on the album. So I had to knock off a few songs so I knocked off "A Day in the Life," or my section of it, and whatever we were talking about, "Mr Kite." Like that. I was very paranoid

VOX

The Toronto Rock and Roll Revival

in those days, I could hardly move.

I read a little interview around when you went to the Rock and Roll Revival in Toronto and you said you were throwing up before you went on stage.

Yeah, yeah, I was. I just threw up for hours until I went on. Nearly threw up during "Cold Turkey" . . . I read a review in *Rolling Stone* about the film of it—which I haven't seen yet, but I'm going to see it tomorrow—and they were saying I was this and that, and I was throwing up nearly in the number. I could hardly sing any of them. I was full of shit.

Would you still be that nervous if you appeared in public?

Always that nervous, but what with one thing and another it just had to come out some way. I don't think I'll do much appearing, it's not worth the strain. I don't want to perform too much for people.

What do you think of George's album [All Things Must Pass]*?*

I don't know . . . I think it's all right, you know. Personally, at home, I wouldn't play that kind of music but I don't want to hurt George's feelings. I don't know how to say about it. I think it's better than Paul's.

What did you think of Paul's [McCartney]*?*

I thought Paul's was rubbish. I think he'll make a better one when he's frightened into it. But I thought that first one was just a lot of . . . I told you, light and whatever, you know that crack. But when I listen to the radio and I hear George's stuff coming over, well then it's pretty bloody good. It's like that, my personal tastes are very strange.

What are your personal tastes?

Wop bop a loo bop. I like rock and roll, man, I don't like much else.

VOX
VOX

Dylan (an evaluation)

Why rock and roll?

That's the music that inspired me to play music. There is nothing conceptually better than rock and roll. No group, be it Beatles, Dylan or Stones has ever improved on "A Whole Lot A Shakin" for my money. Or maybe I'm like our parents, you know, that's my period and I dig it, and I'll never leave it.

What do you think of the rock and roll scene today?

I don't know what it is . . . You would have to name it. I don't think there is . . .

Do you get any pleasure out of the Top Ten? Do you listen to the Top Ten?

No, I never listen. Only when I'm recording or about to bring something out, I'll listen. Just before I record, I go buy a few albums to see what people are doing, if they improved any or what, if anything happened. And nothing's really happened. There's a lot of great guitarists and musicians around, but nothing's happening. I mean I don't like the Blood, Sweat & Tears shit. I think all that is bullshit. And rock and roll is going like jazz as far as I can see, and the bullshitters are going off into that excellentness which I never believed in and others are going off . . . I consider myself in the avant-garde of rock and roll. I don't know, because I'm with . . . Yoko taught me a lot and I taught her a lot and I think on her album you can hear it.

What do you think of Dylan's album, New Morning*?*

I thought it wasn't much. Because I expect more. Maybe I expect too much from people, you know, but I expect more . . . But I haven't been a Dylan follower since he stopped rocking. I liked "Rolling Stone" and a few things he did then. I like a few things he did in the early days but the rest of it is just like Lennon-McCartney or something. It's no different, it's a myth.

"We believed the Beatles myth, too."

You don't think then it's a legitimate new morning?

No, that's a lot of bullshit. It might be a new morning for him because he stopped singing on the top of his voice up there and he's singing down there. I mean it's all right, but I'd sooner have "I Hear You Knocking" by Dave Edmonds. It's the top of England now. (Sings) "You went away and left me, a long time ago . . ."

It's strange that George comes out with this Hare Krishna LP . . .

Yes, yes.

. . . and you come out with the opposite. How do you think he'll react to that?

I don't know. I can't imagine what George thinks. Well I suppose he thinks I've lost the way or something like that. But to me I'm like home. I'll never change much from this.

Always the Beatles were talked about and the Beatles talked about themselves as being four parts of the same person.

Well, to make up . . . yes.

What's happened to those four parts?

They remembered that they were four individuals. You see we believed the Beatles myth, too. I don't know whether the others still believe it. We were four guys . . . I met Paul and said 'You want to join me band?' you know. Then George joined and then Ringo joined. We were just a band who made it very, very big, that's all. Our best work was never recorded.

Why?

Because we were performers—in spite of what Mick says about us—in Liverpool, Hamburg and other dance halls and what we generated was fantastic, where we played straight rock, and there was nobody to touch us in Britain. As soon as we made it, we made it, but the edges were

Self-rating as guitarist

knocked off. Brian put us in suits and all that and we made it very, very big. But we sold out, you know. The music was dead before we even went on the theatre tour of Britain. We were feeling shit already because we had to reduce an hour or two hours playing, which we were glad about in one way, to twenty minutes and go on and repeat the same twenty minutes every night. The Beatles' music died then as musicians. That's why we never improved as musicians. We killed ourselves then to make it. And that was the end of it. George and I are more inclined to say that. We always missed the club dates because that's when we were playing music. And then later on we became technically efficient recording artists, which was another thing. We were competent people, you know and whatever media you put us in we can produce something worthwhile.

How do you rate yourself as a guitarist?

Well, it depends on what kind of guitarist . . .

Rock and roll.

I'm okay. I'm not technically very good, but I can make it fucking howl and move. I was rhythm guitarist. It's an important job. I can make a band drive.

How do you rate George?

He's pretty good. Ha, ha. I prefer myself. I have to be honest, you know. I'm really very embarrassed about my guitar playing in one way because it's very poor. I can never move, but I can make a guitar speak, you know. I think there's a guy called Richie Valens—no, Richie Havens. Does he play very strange guitar? He's a black guy that was on Isle of Wight concert and sang "Strawberry Fields" or something.

Richie Havens.

Opposite: Liverpool, 1962, and on stage, 1964

Yeah, he plays like one chord all the time. He plays pretty funky guitar, but he doesn't seem

"I'm a cinema verité guitarist"

to be able to play in the technical sense at all. I'm like that. Yoko has made me get cocky about my guitar. You see, one part of me says, 'Yes, of course I can play because I can make a rock move.' But the other part of me says, 'Well, I wish I could just do it like BB King.' If you put me with BB, I would feel silly. I'm an artist and if you give me a tuba I'll bring you something out of it.

You say you can make the guitar speak. What songs have you done that on?

"I Found Out." I think it's nice. It drives along. It's . . . I don't know . . . ask Eric Clapton, he thinks I can play, ask him. You don't have to . . . you see a lot of you people . . . want technical things, then you think that's . . . it's like wanting technical films. Most critics of rock and roll, and guitarists, are in the stage of the Fifties where they wanted a technically perfect film, finished for them, and then they would feel happy. I'm a cinema verite guitarist. I'm a musician and you have to break down your barriers to be able to hear what I'm playing. There's a nice little bit I played, they had it on the back of *Abbey Road.* Paul gave us each a piece. There is a little break where Paul plays, George plays and I play. And you listened to it. And there is one bit, one of those where it stops, one of those "Carry That Weight" where it suddenly goes boom, boom on the drums and then we all take it in turns to play. I'm the third one on it. I have a definite style of playing. I've always had. I was overshadowed. They call George the invisible singer, well, I'm the invisible guitarist.

You said you played the obbligato on "Get Back."

I played the solo on that, yeah. When Paul was feeling kindly he would give me a solo. Maybe if he was feeling guilty that he had most of the A-sides or something he'd give me a solo. And I played the solo on that. I think George produces some beautiful guitar playing. But I think he's too hung up to really let go, but so is Eric, really. Maybe he's changed. They're all so hung up, you know. Well, we all are, that's the problem. I really like BB King.

Do you like Ringo's record, his country one?

I think it's a good record. I wouldn't buy any of it, you know. I think it's a good record and I was pleasantly surprised to hear "Beaucoups of Blues." I felt good, I was glad, and I wasn't . . . I didn't feel as embarrassed as I did about his first record.

It's hard for me . . . to ask me, it's like asking me what do I think of . . . ask me about other people, you know, because it looks so awful when I say I don't like this and I don't like that. It's just that I wouldn't . . . I don't like many of the Beatles records, either. My own taste is different from that which I've played sometimes, which is called cop out, to make money, or whatever. Or because I didn't know any better.

Watching *Let It Be*

I would like to ask some more questions about Paul and go through that. We went to see Let It Be *in San Francisco. What was your feeling about that?*

I felt sad. That film was set up by Paul for Paul. That's one of the main reasons the Beatles ended. 'Cause—I can't speak for George, but I pretty damn well know—we got fed up of being side men for Paul. After Brian died, that's what happened, began to happen to us. The camera-work was set up to show Paul and not to show anybody else. And that's how I felt about it. And on top of that, the people that cut it cut it as 'Paul is God' and we're just lyin' around there. That's what I felt. And I knew there were some shots of Yoko, and me, that had been just

chopped out of the film for no other reason than the people were oriented towards Engelbert Humperdinck, and that's . . . I felt sick.

The death of Brian Epstein

How would you trace the breakup of the Beatles?

After Brian died we collapsed. Paul took over and supposedly led us. But what is leading us when we went round in circles? We broke up then. That was the disintegration.

When did you first feel that the Beatles had broken up? When did that idea first hit you?

I don't remember. I was in my own pain. I wasn't noticing really. I just did it like a job. The Beatles broke up after Brian died. We made the double album, the set . . . it's like if you took each track off and gave it all mine and all George's . . . it's just like I told you many times, it was just me and a backing group, Paul and a backing group . . . And I enjoyed it, but we broke up then.

Where were you when you heard Brian died?

We were in Wales with Maharishi. We had just gone down after seeing his lecture the first night and we went down to Wales. We heard it and then we went right off into the Maharishi thing.

Were you in a hotel, or what?

We were just outside a lecture hall with Maharishi, and I don't know . . . I can't remember. I just sort of came over, somebody came up to us . . . the press were there because we had gone down with this strange Indian, you know, and they said Brian's dead. And we, I was stunned, and we all were, I suppose, and the Maharishi, we went in to him, 'What?' you know, 'He's dead,' and all that. And he was sort of saying, 'Oh, forget it, be happy,' fuckin' idiot. You know, like parents, smile, that's what Maharishi said. And we did. We went along with the Maharishi

Opposite: B.B. King

Paul carries on

trip.

What was your feeling when Brian died?

The feeling that anybody has when somebody close to them dies. There is a sort of little hysterical, sort of hee, hee, I'm glad it's not me, or something in it, you know? That funny feeling when somebody dies. I don't know whether you've had it, I've had a lot of people die on me. And the other feeling is What? What the fuck! You know, what can I do? I knew that we were in trouble then. I didn't really have any misconceptions about our ability to do anything other than play music and I was scared. I thought, 'we've fuckin' had it.'

What were the events that immediately happened after Brian died?

Well, we went with Maharishi . . . I remember being in Wales. And then . . . I can't remember I will probably have to have a bloody primal to remember this. I don't remember, you know. It just all happened.

And then you went to India?

Yes, I think so.

How did Paul react?

I don't know how the others took it. You can never tell . . . it's no good asking me . . . it's like asking me how you took it, you know, I don't know. I'm in me own head. I can't be in anybody else's. I don't know really what George, Paul or Ringo think any more than I do about, you know. I know them pretty well, but I don't know anybody that well. Yoko I know about the best. I don't know how they felt. It was my own thing. We were all just dazed.

So Brian died and then you said then what happened is Paul started to take over.

Opposite:
Brian Epstein

I don't know how much of this I want to put out. I think Paul had an impression, he has it

now like a parent, that we should be thankful for what he did for keeping the Beatles going. But when you look upon it objectively, he kept it going for his own sake. Was it for my sake Paul struggled? But Paul made an attempt to carry on as if Brian hadn't died by saying, 'Now, now, boys, we're going to make a record,' you know, and being the kind of person I am, I thought well, we're going to make a record all right, so I went along and we went and made a record. And I suppose we made *Pepper* I'm not sure.

No, that was before.

That was before Brian, oh, I see . . . well, we made the double album then. But it was like that, . . . Was *Magical Mystery Tour* after Brian? . . . Yeah, well, that was the real . . . you see, Paul had a tendency to come along and say, well he's written his ten songs, let's record now. And I said, well, give us a few days and I'll knock a few off or something like that. *Magical Mystery Tour* was not that very . . . he set it up and he had worked it out with Mal and then he came and showed me what his idea was and this is how it went, it went around like this, the story and how he had it all, the production and everything. He said, 'Well, here's the segment, you write a little piece for that.' And I thought, fuckin' Ada, I've never made a film, what's he mean, write a script. So I ran off and wrote the dream sequence for the fat woman and all the things with the spaghetti and all that. It was like that. And then George and I were sort of grumbling, you know, 'Fuckin' movie, oh well, we better do it,' feeling that we owed the public . . . that we should do these things. So we made it.

When did your songwriting partnership with Paul end?

That ended . . . I don't know, around 1962, or something, I don't know. If you give me the albums I can tell you exactly who wrote what, you know, and which line. We sometimes wrote together and sometimes didn't, but all our best work, apart from the early days like "I Want to Hold Your Hand" we wrote together, and things like that we wrote apart, always. The "One After 909" on the whatsit LP is one I wrote when I was 17 or 18 and they were done separately from Paul and some of his were things Paul wrote separately. We always wrote separately, but we wrote together because we enjoyed it a lot sometimes and also because they would say, well, you're going to make an album, we'd get together and knock off a few songs, just like a job.

The Maharishi Mahesh Yogi

Whose idea was it to go to India?

I don't know . . . I don't know, probably George's, I have no idea. Yoko and me, we met around then. I was gonna take her. I lost me nerve because I was going to take me ex-wife and Yoko and I didn't know how to work it. So I didn't quite do it.

"Sexy Sadie" you wrote about the Maharishi?

That's about the Maharishi, yes. I copped out and I wouldn't write "Maharishi what have you done, you made a fool of everyone," but now it can be told, Fab Listeners.

When did you realize that he was making a fool of you?

I don't know, I just sort of saw him.

While in India or when you got back?

Yes, there was a big hullabaloo about him trying to rape Mia Farrow and trying to get off with Mia Farrow and a few other women and things like that. And we went down to him after we stayed up all night discussing 'was it true or not true.' When George started thinking it might be true, I thought well, it must be true, because if George is doubting him, there must be something in it.

So we went to see Maharishi, the whole gang of us the next day charged down to his hut, his bungalow, his very rich-looking bungalow in the mountains. I was the spokesman, and as usual, when the dirty work came, I actually had to be leader—wherever the scene was when it came to the nitty gritty I had to do the speaking. And I said 'We're leaving.' He asked 'Why?' and all that shit, and I said 'Well, if you're so cosmic, you'll know why,' because he was always intimating, and there were all these right-hand men intimating that he did miracles, you know. And I said 'You know why,' and he said 'I don't know why, you must tell me,' and I just kept saying 'You ought to know,' and he gave me a look like 'I'll kill you, you bastard,' and he gave me such a look and I knew then, when he looked at me, you know, because I had called his bluff, because I said if you know all, you know. Cosmic consciousness, that's what we're all here for. I was a bit rough to him.

Yoko: You expected too much from him.

John: I always do, I always expect too much. I was always expecting my mother and don't get her, that's what it is, you know, or some parents, I know that much.

When did you decide that you had to come to New York and denounce the Maharishi?

Denounce him?

Well, you came to New York and had that press conference.

The Apple thing. That was to announce Apple.

But also at the same time you said something about the Maharishi.

I don't remember that. Well, what did I say?

Opposite:
The Maharishi
(and Brian Jones)

"I walked in and changed everything"

I don't know. You know we all say a lot of things that we don't know what we're talking about, I'm probably doing it now. I don't know what I say. You see everybody takes you up on the words you said, you see, and I'm just a guy who people ask what about things and I blab off and some of it makes sense and some of it is bullshit and some of it is lies and some of it is God knows what I'm saying. I don't know what I said about Maharishi, all I know was we said about Apple, which was worse.

Will you talk about Apple?

All right.

How did that start?

Clive Epstein, or some other such business freak, came up to us and said you've got to spend so much money or the tax will take you. We're thinking of opening some retail . . . it wasn't record shops, a chain of retail clothes or some balmy thing like that and we were all muttering about, well, if we are going to have to open a shop, let's open something we're interested in. And we went through all these different ideas about this, that and the other, and we ended up with a . . . Paul had a nice idea about opening up a white house where we would sell white china and things like that, everything white, you know, because you can never get anything white, you know, which was pretty groovy, and it didn't end up with that. It ended up with Apple and all this junk and The Fool and all the stupid clothes and all that.

When did you decide to close that down?

I don't know. I was controlling the scene at the time. I mean I was the one going in the office and shouting about. Paul had done it for six months, I walked in and changed everything. And there were all the Peter Browns reporting behind my back to Paul saying, 'You know John's doing this and he's doing that and like John's crazy.' I was always the one that must be crazy because I wouldn't let them have status quo. (To Yoko:) Was it my idea or yours? Well, we came up with the idea to give it all away and stop fuckin' about with a psychedelic clothes shop. So we gave it all away. It was a good happening.

Returning the MBE

Were you there for the give-away?

No, we read it in the papers. That was when we started events. I learned events from Yoko. Events we did—we made everything into events from then on and got rid of it.

When you gave away your MBE . . .

Yes, I'd been planning on it for over a year and a bit. I was waiting for a time to do it.

. . . you said then that you were waiting to tag it to some event, then you realized that it was an event in itself.

Yes, that's the truth.

You also said at that time you had another thing you were going to do.

I don't know what it was.

Do you remember?

Yes, I do. We had some . . . well we always kept them on their toes, you know, during our events period. I don't know, but we said we have some other surprise for them later. I can't remember what it was. Maybe we were getting married . . . no, we were married . . . no, I don't know.

Yoko: You mean after the baby died?

John: After the MBE we probably intimated that we had another surprise event coming up shortly.

Yoko: Probably the War Is Over poster event.

To go back to Apple for a minute and the break up

of the Beatles, Brian died, and one thing and another . . .

I didn't really want to talk about all this . . . go on.

Do you mind?

Well, we're halfway through it now, so let's do it.

You said you quit the Beatles first.

Yes.

How?

Well, I said to Paul, I'm leaving. We were in Apple, and . . . I knew before we went to Toronto. I told Allen [Klein] I was leaving, I told Eric Clapton and Klaus that I was leaving and that I'd like to probably use them as a group. I hadn't decided how to do it—to have a permanent new group or what, then later on I thought, fuck, I'm not going to get stuck with another set of people, you know, whoever they are. So I announced it to myself and to the people around me on the way to Toronto a few days before. And on the plane, Allen came with me, and I told Allen it's over. When I got back there were a few meetings and Allen had said well, cool it, cool it, 'cause there was a lot to do businesswise, you know, and it would not have been suitable at the time. And then we were discussing something in the office with Paul and Paul said something or other like to do something and I kept saying no, no, no to everything he said, you see. So it came to a point I had to say something, of course, and Paul said 'What do you mean?' I said 'I mean the group is over, I'm leaving.' But Allen was there, and he will remember exactly, and Yoko will, but this is exactly how I see it.

Allen was saying don't tell. He didn't want me to tell Paul even. Well, I couldn't help it, so I said it's out, I couldn't stop it, it came out. Paul and Allen said they were glad that I wasn't going to announce it. Like I was going to make an event out of it. But Paul and Allen both . . . I don't know whether Paul said don't tell anybody but he was damn pleased that I wasn't, you know. He said, 'Oh, well, that means nothing really happened if you're not going to say anything.' So that's what happened.

Paul's reaction

What was Paul's reaction when you said you were leaving?

So, like anybody when you say divorce, you know, their face goes all sorts of colors. It's like he knew, really, that this was the final thing. And then six months later he comes out with whatever. A lot of people knew I left. I was a fool not to do it, not to do what Paul did, which was use it to sell a record.

You were really angry with Paul?

No, I wasn't angry.

Well, when he came out with his 'I'm leaving.'

No I wasn't angry, I was just . . . shit! He's a good PR man, Paul. I mean he's about the best in the world, probably, he really does a job. I wasn't angry, in that way, I was . . . we were all hurt that he didn't tell us what he was going to do. I think he claims that he didn't mean that to happen, but that's bullshit. He called me in the afternoon of that day and said 'I'm doing what you and Yoko were doing last year.' And I said, 'Good,' you know, because last year they were all looking at us as if we were strange trying to make our life together and doing other things than being fab, fat myths. So he rang me up that day and said 'I'm doing what you and Yoko are doing, I'm putting out an album and I'm leaving the group, *too*,' he said. I said good, you know, I was feeling a little strange because *he* was saying it this time although it was a year later, and I said good because he was the one that wanted the Beatles most. And then the midnight papers came out.

How did you feel then?

I was cursing because I hadn't done it. I wanted to do it, I should have done it . . . 'ah, damn, shit, what a fool I was.' But there were many pressures at that time with Northern Songs, all that was going on. It would have upset the whole thing if I would have said that.

How did you feel when you found out that Dick James had sold his shares?

I was pissed off.

Did you feel betrayed?

Sure I did. He's another one of them people, a bit like Martin, who think they made us, you know, and they didn't. I'd like to hear Dick James' music and I'd like to hear George Martin's music, please, just play me some. And Dick James actually has said that, you know.

What?

That he made us. People are under a delusion that they made us when in fact we made them.

How did Dick James tell you that, well, I'm . . .

He didn't tell us, he did it. It was just a fait-accompli, he went and sold his thing to Lew Grade and that's all we knew. We read it in the paper, I think.

What was that part about Lew Grade?

Oh, it was fantastic. It was like this room full of old men smoking and fighting, you know, deciding. It's great. People seem to think that businessmen like Allen or Grade or any of them are a race apart. They play the game the way we play music and it's something to see. They play a game and they have ritual, and they create . . . like Allen, he's a very creative guy. He creates situations which create positions for them to move in. They all do it and it's a sight to see. We played our part, we both did.

"I maneuver people, that's what leaders do"

What did you do?

With the bankers and things like that. I think Allen could tell you better. I forget fragments of it, everything seems as though it's going to be trouble, you know, like you can't say anything about anybody because you get sued, or something. So check Allen with that, he'll tell you what we did. I did a job on this banker that we were using and a few other people, and on the Beatles.

What kind?

How do you describe the job, you know, my job . . . I maneuver people, that's what leaders do. And I sit and make situations which will be of benefit to me with other people. It's as simple as that. I'm maneuvered too. I had to do a job to get Allen in Apple. I did a job, so did you.

Yoko: You do it with instinct, you know.

John: Oh, God, Yoko, don't say that. Maneuvering is what it is. Let's not be coy about it. It's a deliberate and thought-out maneuver of how to get a situation how we want it. That's how life's about, isn't it. Is it not? Isn't it?

Yoko: Well, you're pretty instinctive.

John: Instinctive doesn't . . . so is Allen, so is Dick James, so is Grade. They're all instinctive, so is he, if it's instinct . . . but it's maneuvering, there's nothing ashamed about it, we all do it. It's just owning up, you know, not going around saying 'God bless you, brother, hare fuckin' Krishna,' and doin' it pretending there is no vested interest.

Yoko: The difference is that you don't go down and bullshit and get him, but you just instinctively said that Allen is the guy to jump

Think you're a genius?

into it and you just get him.

John: But that's not the thing. The point I'm talking about is creating a situation around Apple and the Beatles in which Allen could come in. That's what I'm talking about, and he wouldn't have gotten in unless I'd done it. And he wouldn't have gotten in unless you'd done it. You made the decision, too.

How did you get Allen in?

The same as I get anything I want. The same as you get what you want. I'm not telling you; just work at it, get on the phone, a little word here and a little word there and do it.

What was Paul's reaction?

You see a lot of people, all the Dick Jameses, Derek Taylors, and Peter Browns, all of them, they think they're the Beatles, and Neil and all of them. Well, I say fuck 'em, you know; and after working with genius for 10, 15 years they begin to think they're it, you know. They're not.

Do you think you're a genius?

Yes, if there is such a thing as one, I am one.

When did you first realize that?

When I was about twelve. I used to think I must be a genius but nobody's noticed. I used to think whether I'm a genius or I'm mad, which is it? I used to think, well, I can't be mad because nobody's put me away; therefore, I'm a genius. I mean genius is a form of madness and we're all that way. But I used to be a bit coy about it, you know, like me guitar playing, you know. If there is such a thing as genius, which is just what . . . what the fuck is it, I am one, you know, and if there isn't, I don't care. I used to think it when I was a kid, writing me poetry and doing me paintings. I didn't become something when the Beatles made it, or when you heard about me, I've been like this all me life. Genius is pain,

Early reaction to Yoko

too. It's just pain.

How do you feel towards the Beatles people?

Who, the Apple?

Yes, the Apple . . . you talk about Mal and Derek . . .

I didn't mention Mal. I said Neil, Peter Brown and Derek. They live in a dream of Beatle past and everything they do is oriented to that. They also have a warped view of what was happening. I suppose we all do.

They must feel now that their lives are inextricably bound up in yours.

Well, they have to grow up, then. They've only had half their life and they've got another whole half to go, and they can't go on pretending to be Beatles. That's where it's at. They don't know, I mean when they read this they'll think it's cracked John, if it's in the article. But that's where it's at. They live in the past.

You traveled to Toronto with Derek, right?

Yes.

And also did the Bed Peace up there.

That was the same thing, yeah. Well, then I was still living in the past too, then.

You see I presumed that I would just be able to carry on and just bring Yoko into our life. But it seemed that I had to either be married to them or Yoko, and I chose Yoko, and I was right.

What were their reactions when you first brought Yoko by?

They despised her.

From the very beginning?

Yeah, right, and they insulted her and they still do.

Is that Beatle people?

Yeah. They don't even know I can see it, and even when it's written down it will look like I'm just paranoid, or she's paranoid, I know. Just by the way the publicity on us was handled in Apple all of the two years we were together, and the attitude of people to us and the bits we hear from the office girls. We know, so they can go stuff themselves.

"The most big-headed, uptight people on earth"

Yoko: In the beginning we were too much in love to notice anything.

John: Yeah . . . we were in our own dream. But they're the kind of idiots that really think that Yoko split the Beatles probably, or Allen, it's the same joke, really. They are that insane about Allen, too.

How would you characterize George's, Paul's and Ringo's reactions to Yoko?

It's the same. You can quote Paul, you can look in the papers. He said many times that at first he hated Yoko and then he got to like her. It's too late for me, I'm for Yoko, you know. Why should she take that kind of shit from those people. They were writing about her looking miserable in *Let It Be.* You sit through 60 sessions with the most big-headed, uptight people on earth and see what it's fuckin' like, and be insulted by, just because you love someone. And George, shit, insulted her right to her face in the Apple office at the beginning; just being 'straight forward' you know, that game of 'Well, I'm going to be upfront because this is what we've heard, and Dylan, and a few people said she'd got a lousy name in New York, and you give off bad vibes.' That's what George said to her and we both sat through it, and I didn't hit him, I don't know why, but I was always hoping that they would come around.

I couldn't believe it, you know. And they all sat there with their wives, like a fucking jury, and judged us, and the only thing I did was write

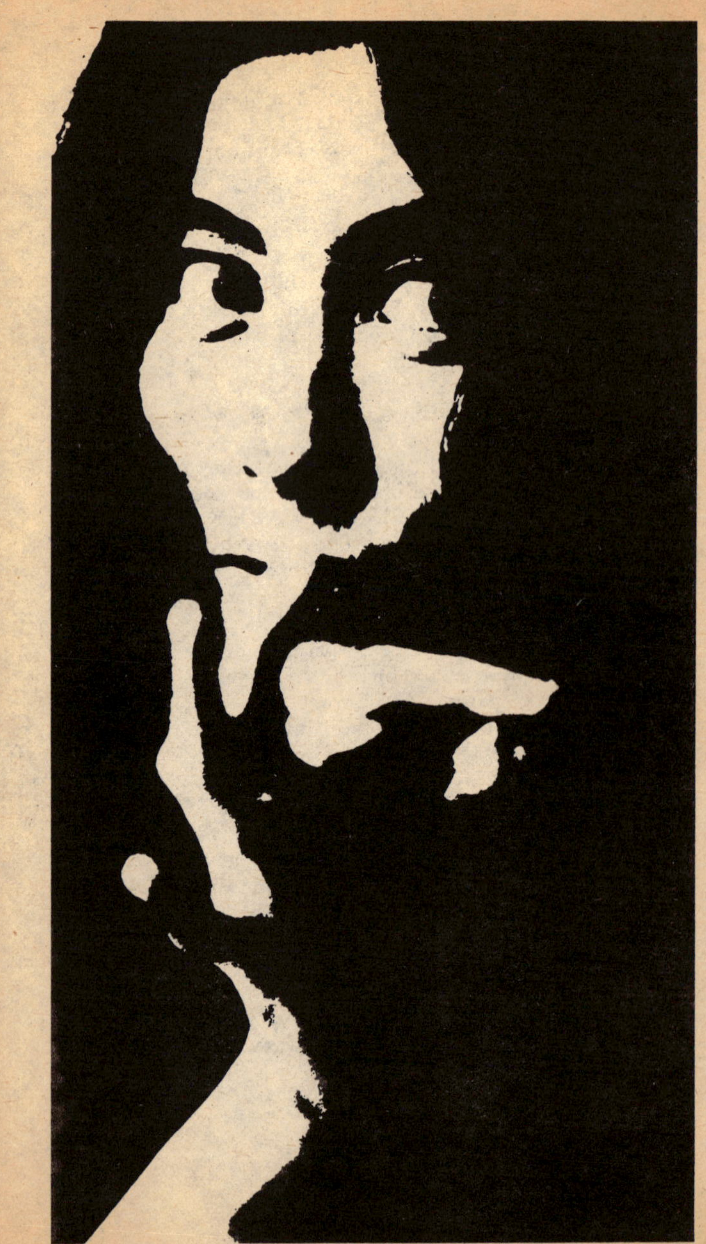

that piece about "some of our beast friends" in my usual way, because I was never honest enough. I always had to write in that gobbledegook. And that's what they did to us. Ringo was all right, so was Maureen, but the other two really gave it to us. I'll never forgive them, I don't care what fuckin' shit about Hare Krishna and God . . . and Paul about 'Well, I've changed me mind,' I can't forgive 'em for that, really; although I can't help still loving them either.

Beatles and the avant-garde

When did you realize that you were just going to be unable to reconcile Paul and George to Yoko?

I don't know when it was . . . when I decided to leave the group. I wanted Yoko . . . Yoko played me tapes I understood. I know it was very strange and avant-garde music is a very tough thing to assimilate and all that, but I've heard the Beatles playing avant-garde music when nobody was looking for years. But they're artists, and all artists have fuckin' big egos, whether they like to admit it or not, and when a new artist came into the group, they were never allowed. Sometimes George and I would like to bring somebody in like Billy Preston, that was exciting, we might have had him in the group. We were fed up with the same old shit, but it wasn't wanted. And I would have expanded the Beatles and broken them if . . . and either get their pants off and stop being God . . . but it didn't work. And Yoko was naive; she came in and she would expect to perform with them like you would with any group. She was jamming, but there would be a sort of coldness about it. I decided to leave the group when I decided that I could no longer artistically get anything out of the Beatles and here was someone that could turn me on to a million things.

How did you choose the musicians you use on this

Early ambitions

record?

I'm a very nervous person, really. I'm not as big-headed as this interview sounds, this is me projecting through the fear. So I choose people that I know rather than strangers.

Like you used Ringo.

Yeah.

Why do you get along with Ringo?

Because in spite of all the things, the Beatles really could play music together when they weren't uptight. And if I get a thing going Ringo knows where to go, just like that, and he does well. We've played together so long that it fits. That's the only thing I sometimes miss is being able to just sort of blink or make a certain noise and I know they'll all know where we are going on an ad lib thing. But I don't miss it that much.

You always said that the Beatles wanted to be bigger than Elvis.

Yes.

Why?

Because Elvis was the biggest. We wanted to be the biggest, doesn't everybody?

When did you decide that?

Well, first of all Paul and I wanted to be the Goffin & King of England. This was an old story because Goffin & King were writing this great stuff at that time, and we decided well, we're better than them, so we want to be this . . . we want to be this, we want to be the next thing, we want to be President, or whatever. It goes on and on and on. But we always wanted to be bigger than Elvis because Elvis was the thing. Whatever people say, he was it.

At what moment did you realize that you were bigger than Elvis?

I don't know. See it's different when it happens, you've forgotten about it. It's like when you

actually get the number one, or whatever it is, it's different. It's the going for it which is the fun.

And then at some point you just never thought about it again?

Yes. We were just like jelly, we sat in a mold and we floated about like that for periods.

You say that the dream is over, and part of the dream was that the Beatles were God and that the Beatles were the messengers of God, and the Beatles had been God, or yourself as God . . .

Yeah, well, if there is a God, we're all it.

When did you first start getting the reactions from people who listened to the records . . . the first sort of spiritual reaction?

This record? There is a guy in England called William Mann who writes in the *Times* who was the first intellectual reviewer of the Beatles, which got people talking about us in that intellectual way.

As musicians?

Yeah, he wrote about aeolian cadences and all sorts of musical terms, and he is a bullshitter. But he made us credible with intellectuals. And he wrote about Paul's album as if it was written by Beethoven or something; this last one—he was just voted Album of the Year and all that shit, you know. He's still writing the same shit. But it did us a lot of good in that way because people in all the middle classes and intellectuals are all going 'Ooooh.'

When did somebody first come up to you about this thing about John Lennon as God?

I didn't know what to do . . . like 'you tell us, guru,' that bit? . . . probably after acid. I don't know, *Rubber Soul* . . . I can't remember. I can't remember it exactly happening. We just took that position. I mean we started putting out messages. Like "The word is Love" and things like that. I write messages.

LSD (introduction to)

Yoko: "Strawberry Fields" is a message.

John: Oh that's later on, this is earlier on. See, when you start putting out messages people start asking you what's the message.

How did you first get involved in LSD?

A dentist in London laid it on George, me and our wives without telling us at a dinner party at his house. He was a friend of George's, and our dentist at the time, and he just put it in our coffee or something. And we went . . . and he was saying I advise you not to . . . he didn't know what it was, it's all the thing with that sort of . . . middle-class London swingers, or whatever, had all heard about it and they didn't know it was different from pot or pills. And they gave us it and he was saying I advise you not to leave, and we thought he was trying to keep us for an orgy in his house and we didn't want to know. And we went out to the Ad Lib and these discotheques, and there were these incredible things going on. And that's how it happened.

Around his table?

No, this was the dinner, and we got out and this guy came with us and he was nervous and we didn't know what was going on and that we were going crackers. It was insane going around London on it. And we thought, when we went to the club, it was on fire, and then we thought it was a premiere and it was just an ordinary light outside. We thought, shit, what's going on here. And we were cackling in the streets, and then people were shouting let's break a window. We were just insane. We were just out of our heads. People would come up to me . . . we finally got on the lift. We all thought there was a fire on the lift, there was just a little red light, we were

"I was pretty stunned . . ."

all screaming aaaaaaagh, like that, and we were all hot and hysterical. And we all arrived on the floor, because this was a discotheque that was up a building, and the lift stops, and the door opens, and we were all aaaaaaaagh. And we just see that it's the club, and we walk in and sit down and the table's elongating. I think we went to eat before that and it was like in the thing I read about opium where the table . . . I suddenly realized it was only a table, like this, with four of us 'round it, but it went this long, just like I had read—describing the effects of opium in the old days, and I thought 'Fuck! it's happening.' And then we went to the Ad Lib and all of that, and then some singer came up to me and said can I sit next to you and I said only if you don't talk, because I just couldn't think.

When you came down what did you think?

I was pretty stunned for a month or two.

Where did you go after that?

Well, it seemed to go on all night. I can't remember the details, it just went on. And George somehow or other managed to drive us home in his Mini, but we were going about 10 miles an hour, it seemed like a thousand. And Patty was saying let's jump out and play football, there were these big Rugby poles and things like that. And I was getting all these sort of hysterical jokes coming out like speed, because I was always on that, too. George was going 'Don't make me laugh, Oh God!' It was just terrifying, but it was fantastic. I did some drawings at the time, I've got them somewhere, of four faces saying 'We all agree with you!' you know, things like that. I gave them to Ringo, the originals. I did a lot of drawing that night. And then George's house seemed to be, you know, just like a big submarine. I was driving it, they all went to bed. I was carrying on in it, it seemed to float above his wall, which was eighteen foot, and I was driving it. The second time we had it in LA was different.

LSD (in California)

What happened then?

Well, then we took it deliberately.

Back track a second, after everybody slept . . .

I don't remember, you know, it was just . . .

Everybody got up . . .

Then later, I can't remember, we were all just a bit down, you know, and felt 'Wow!' I don't remember that kind of thing, I only remember the highlights. And then, well, we just decided to take it again in California.

Where were you?

We were on tour in one of those houses like Doris Day's house, or whatever it was we used to stay in, and the three of us took it, Ringo, George and I, and I think maybe Neil and a couple of the Byrds, that what's-his-name, the one in the Stills and Nash thing, you know. The Byrds, Crosby and the other guy, who used to do the lead, McGuinn, I think they came, I'm not sure, on a few trips. But there was a reporter, Don Short . . . when we were in the garden, it was only our second one, we still didn't know anything about doing it in a nice place and cool it and all that, we just took it. Then we suddenly saw the reporter and thought how do we act normal; we imagined we acted extraordinarily, which we weren't. We thought surely somebody could see. We were terrified waiting for him to go and he wondered why he couldn't come over. And Neil, who never had acid either, had taken it, and he still had to play road manager, and we said go and get rid of Don Short, and he didn't know what to do, he just sort of sat with it. And Peter Fonda came, and that was another

"She Said, She Said"

thing, and he kept saying in a whisper 'I know what it's like to be dead,' and we said 'What?' and he kept saying it. We were saying 'For Chrissake shut up, we don't care, we don't want to know' and he kept going on about it. And that's how I wrote "She said, she said, I know what it's like to be dead."

What else turned into that song?

"She Said, She Said"?

Yeah.

Well, it was a sad song. It was just an acidy song, I suppose. "And when I was a little boy," you see . . . a lot of early childhood was coming out, anyway.

How long did LSD go on?

It went on for years. I must have had a thousand trips.

Literally a thousand or a couple of hundred?

Lots. I used to just eat it all the time.

Through what albums?

I don't know. I never took it in the studio. Once I did, actually, I thought I was taking some uppers and I was not in the state of handling it. And I can't remember what album it was, but I took it and I just noticed . . . I suddenly got so scared on the mike, I said what is it, I feel ill. I thought I felt ill and I thought I was going cracked. I said I must get some air. They all took me upstairs on the roof and George Martin was looking at me funny, and then it dawned on me I must have taken acid. I said, well, I can't go on, I have to go, so I just said you'll have to do it and I'll just stay and watch. I got very nervous just watching them all, and I kept saying, 'Is it all right?' They were saying yeah, and they had all been very kind and they said yes, it's all right. I said are you sure it's all right. They carried on making the record.

Bad trips

The other Beatles didn't get into LSD as much as you did?

George did pretty . . . in LA, the second time we took it, Paul felt very out of it because we were all a bit slightly cruel, sort of 'we're taking it, and you're not.' But we kept *seeing* him, you know. And we couldn't eat our food, I just couldn't manage it, we were just picking it up with our hands and there were all these people sort of serving us in the house, and that, we were just sort of knocking food on the floor and all of that. It was a long time before Paul took it. And then there was the big announcement.

Right.

So I think George was pretty heavy on it, we are probably both the most cracked. Paul is a bit more stable than George and I.

And straight?

I don't know about straight—stable. I think LSD profoundly shocked him and Ringo. I think maybe they regret it.

Did you have many bad trips?

Oh, yeah, I had many, Jesus Christ, I stopped taking it because of that, you know. I just couldn't stand it.

You got too afraid to take it?

Yeah, it got like that. But then I dropped it for I don't know how long. And then I started taking it again just before I met Yoko. Derek came over and . . . you see I got the wrong . . . I got a message on acid that you should destroy your ego, and I did, you know. I was reading that stupid book of Leary's and all that shit. We were going through a whole game that everybody went through, and I destroyed myself. And I was slowly putting myself together round about Maharishi time, and bit by bit over a two-year period. And I destroyed me ego and I didn't believe I could do anything, and I let people do what they wanted and say—let them all just do what they wanted, and I just was nothing, I was shit. And then Derek tripped me out at his house after he got back from LA. He said . . . he said it's all . . . he sort of said 'you're all right' and he pointed out which songs I had written and he said 'you wrote this, and you said this and you are intelligent, don't be frightened.' And then next week I went down with Yoko and we tripped again, and she filled me completely to realize that I was me, and that it's all right. And that was it, and I started fighting again and being a loudmouth again, and saying, well, I can do this, and fuck you, this is what I want, you know, I want it and don't put me down, I did this. So that's where I am now.

How do you think that affected your conception of the music, in general?

Well it was only another mirror, it didn't . . . it wasn't a miracle. It was more of a visual thing, and a therapy, that 'looking at yourself' bit, you know. It did all that. I don't quite remember, you know, you don't only hear the music, but it didn't write the music, neither did Janov or Maharishi in the same terms. I write the music in the circumstances in which I'm in, whether it's on acid or in the water.

Yoko: And in all those trips you just didn't lose yourself.

"She Said, She Said" would be like the first song you wrote that had something connected with it, an influential drug experience?

No, not really. There is nothing I can pinpoint because, I mean like *Rubber Soul* was pot, or the one before with the white drawing on it. You know, it was like pills influenced us in Hamburg, drink influenced us in so and so and, I don't know, there are no specific things. I only wrote because the guy said I know what it's like to be dead. I thought that was . . . if I had read it in the paper I would have written a song about it. And to write a mood song, if I'm sad, I would just write sort of sad things, just remember sad things like 'when I was a boy everything was right,' and all that, which was a dream. I would put myself in a sad mood and write a sad song, or be in a sad mood and write a song in more like it.

What did you think when you saw A Hard Day's Night?

Well, I thought it wasn't bad. It could have been better. You see there's another illusion that we were just puppets and that these great people like Brian Epstein and Dick Lester created the situation and made this whole fuckin' thing. But it was really precisely because we were what we were, and realistic, we didn't want to make a fuckin' shitty pop movie. We didn't even want to make a movie that was going to be bad, and we insisted on having a real writer to write it. And Brian came up with Allen Owen, from Liverpool, who had written a play for TV called *No Trams to Lime Street* which I knew, and I think maybe Paul knew, and maybe they all knew *No Trams to Lime Street.* Lime Street is a famous street in Liverpool where the whores used to be in the old days, and he was famous for writing Liverpool dialogue. And we auditioned people to write for us. And they came up with this guy and we knew his work and we said all right, but then he had to come 'round with us to see what we were like. But he was a bit phoney. He was like a professional Liverpool man, like a professional American. He stayed with us two days and wrote the whole thing based on our characters then:

"It wasn't realistic enough"

me, witty; Ringo, dumb and cute; George, this; Paul, that. We were a bit infuriated by the glibness of it and the shittyness of the dialogue. And we were always trying to get it more realistic, even with Dick and all that, and make the camerawork more realistic, but they wouldn't have it. But they made that movie and so that's how it happened. It was OK but the next one was just bullshit, although Dick Lester's comic strip 'Batman' idea in *Help* was ahead of its time.

My impression of the movie was that it was you and it wasn't anyone else.

It was a good projection of one facade of us, which was on tour, once in London and once in Dublin. It was of us in that situation together, in a hotel, having to perform before people. We were like that . . . Allen Owen saw the press conference, so he recreated it in the movie. He recreated it pretty well, but we thought it was phoney then, even. It wasn't realistic enough.

Were you aware of the impact that A Hard Day's Night *had in the States? I mean other than being tremendously popular?*

I don't remember, all we knew was big hit or no hit. I don't remember anything else.

Well, all the American musicians, you might say, they went and saw A Hard Day's Night *and realized rock and roll was OK.*

I see, I see. No, I was never aware of those impacts. We knew it was better than other rock movies, I was aware of musical impacts more, listening to . . . I knew he got that from us, and we got that from . . . and all that kind of thing.

What else have you heard?

Oh, I can just tell where the groups came from, and all that, any of them now. I can tell, you know, like Zeppelin and Fleetwood Mac, you can hear where everything came from. The same as

Opposite: from the film *Help*

Drugs and music (continued)

you can with anybody, you know.

I remember this single coming out "Day Tripper"/ "We Can Work It Out."

That was a drug song, in a way.

"Day Tripper"?

Yes.

Why?

Because it was a day tripper. I just liked the word.

At some point, right in there between Help *and* A Hard Day's Night *you got into drugs and got into doing drug songs.*

Help was made on pot, *A Hard Day's Night* I was on pills. That's drugs, that's bigger drugs than pot. I've been on pills since I was fifteen, no, since I was seventeen or nineteen . . . since I became a musician. The only way to survive in Hamburg to play eight hours a night was to take pills. The waiters gave you them . . . the pills and drink. I was a fucking dropped down drunk in art school. *Help* was where we turned on to pot and dropped drink, simple as that. I've always needed a drug to survive. The others too, but I always had more. I always took more pills, more of everything because I'm more crazy probably.

When did you first start writing message songs, serious songs?

Probably after dinner, I don't know. "Day Tripper" wasn't a serious message song.

I don't mean serious message song in that sense, I mean there was a big change in your music from "You Can't Buy Me Love" to "We Can Work It Out."

I suppose it was pot then. "We Can Work It Out" was . . . Paul wrote that chorus, I wrote the middle bit about "Life is very short, there is no time for fussing and fighting . . ." all that bit. I don't remember any change-over. Other than when you take pot you're a little more less aggressive than when you take alcohol. When you're on alcohol and pills, you just couldn't remember anything.

Can you tell me if that white album with the drawing by Klaus Voorhman on it was before *Rubber Soul* or after?

After. You really don't remember which?

No. Maybe the others do. I don't remember those kinds of things because it doesn't mean anything. It's all gone.

Well, Rubber Soul *was the first attempt to do a serious—*

We were just getting better, technically and musically, that's all. We finally took over the studio. In the early days we had to take what we were given, we had to make it in two hours or whatever it was, and one or three takes was enough, and we didn't know how you can get more bass. We were learning the technique. On *Rubber Soul*, we were sort of more precise about making the album, that's all, and we took over the cover and everything.

What was Rubber Soul, *that was just a simple play on—*

That was Paul's title. It was like "Yer Blues," I suppose, meaning English soul, "Rubber Soul," I suppose, just a pun. There is no great mysterious meaning behind all of this, it was just four boys, you know, working out what to call a new album.

Why did Derek and Brian have a big fall out?

Derek is another egomaniac. And Brian was very hard to live with, he had a lot of tantrums and things like that, like most fags do, you know, they are very insecure. Some things happened which I don't remember, maybe Paul or somebody would, you'd have to ask them. They had many arguments and Derek would walk out be-

"Like Fellini's *Satyricon*"

cause he was too proud to do certain jobs. That's the same now, and I don't blame him, but don't get paid for it. So that's what happened, they had a big row. Derek was hired by Brian, so was Peter Brown, they really were not hired by us. We hired Neil in Liverpool and Mal in Liverpool, those were the only people we ever hired.

The Hunter Davies book says . . .

It was bullshit.

The Hunter Davies book?

Well, it was really bullshit. You know, it was written in the sort of 'Sunday Times' . . . the Fab Four. And no home truths were written, my auntie knocked all the truth bits from my childhood and my mother out and I allowed it, which was my cop out, etc, etc. There was nothing about the orgies and the shit that happened on tour, and I wanted a real book to come out, but we all had wives and didn't want to hurt their feelings. End of that one. Because they still have. You know, the Beatles' tours were like Fellini's *Satyricon.* I mean we had that image, but man, our tours were like something else. If you could get on our tours, you were in. They were *Satyricon*, all right.

Set the scene without names . . .

Yeah . . . Australia, what, just everywhere. Just *Satyricon.* Just think of *Satyricon* with four musicians going through it.

Would you go to a town . . . a hotel?

Wherever we went there was always a whole scene going. We had our four bedrooms separate from . . . tried to keep them out of our room. And Derek's and Neil's rooms were always full of fuck knows what, and policemen and everything. *Satyricon!* We had to do something, and what do you do when the pill doesn't wear off, when it's time to go. I used to be up all night

Opposite: Fellini's *Satyricon*

"The police escorted me to the places"

with Derek, whether there was anybody there or not. I could never sleep, such a heavy scene it was. Like everyone . . . they're all doing it now . . . they didn't call them groupies then, they called it something else. If we couldn't get groupies, we would have whores and everything, whatever was going.

Like businessmen on a convention.

Oh sure it was. When we hit town, we hit it, we were not pissing about. You know there's photographs of me groveling about, crawling about in Amsterdam on my knees, coming out of whore houses and things like that, and people saying 'Good morning, John,' and all of that. And the police escorted me to the places, and things like that, because they never wanted a big scandal. I don't really want to talk about it because it will hurt Yoko, and it's not fair. Suffice to say, just put it like they were *Satyricon* on tour and that's it, because I don't want to hurt the other people's girls either, it's just not fair, I'm sorry.

Yoko: I was surprised. I really didn't know things like that. I thought, well, John is an artist and probably he had two or three affairs before getting married. That is the concept you have in the old school, New York artists group, you know, that kind.

The generation gap.

Yoko: Right, right, exactly.

Let me ask you about something about you and Brian.

Ah, fuck knows what was said. I was pretty close to Brian because if somebody is going to manage me I want to know them inside out. And there was a period when he told me he was a fag. I hate the way Allen is attacked and Brian is made like an angel just because he's dead. He wasn't, you know, he was just a guy.

What else about that Hunter Davies book that you

don't . . .

That I don't know, because I can't remember it. *Love Me Do* was a better book, by Michael Brown on the Beatles. That was a true book. He wrote how we were, which was bastards. You can't be anything else in a situation of such pressurized . . . and we took it out on people like Neil, Derek and Mal; and that's why, underneath their facade, they resent us, but they can never show it and they won't believe it when they read it if it's in print, etc, but they took a lot of shit from us because we were in such a shitty position. It was hard work and somebody had to take it. Those things are left out, you know, about what bastards we were. Fuckin' big bastards, that's what the Beatles were. You have to be a bastard to make it, and that's a fact. And the Beatles are the biggest bastards on earth. Like Allen's Christmas card says: 'Yea, though I walk through the Valley of the Shadow of Death, I will fear no evil, because I'm the biggest bastard in the valley,' or something like that. There's no kidding, if you make it, you're a bastard.

"The Authorized Biography"—image and reality

YOKO: How did you manage to keep that clean image. It's amazing.

JOHN: Because everybody wants the image to carry on. The press around with you, you want to carry on, because they want the free drinks and the free whores and the fun. Everybody wants to keep on the bandwagon. It's *Satyricon.* We were the Caesars. Who was going to knock us when there's a million pounds to be made? All the hand-outs, the bribery, the police, all the fucking hype, you know. Everybody wanted in, that's why some of them are still trying to cling on to this. Don't take it away from us, you know, don't take Rome from us, not a portable Rome where we can all have our houses and our cars

Early days in London

and our lovers and our wives and office girls and parties and drink and drugs. Don't take it from us, you know, otherwise you're mad, John, you're crazy. Silly John wants to take all this away.

What do you say to Beatle people today?

What do you mean, like Beatle fans?

Yes.

It depends on who they are. If they ask me something about *A Hard Day's Night* or *Help*, I'm just straight with them and say it was good fun, or it was like this. I'm giving you the dirt but a lot of it was great fun. I don't meet any Beatle people, do I? I don't know where they are. In fact, I don't really know how to answer that. Those Apple Scruffs, or whatever, I mean, I don't know what they are, Beatle people or not.

By Beatle people . . . there is something I would really like to get back to about what you said about the dream being over.

I'm saying like what Dylan said, don't follow leaders. He said it once.

What was it like in the early days in London?

When we came down we were treated like real provincials by the Londoners. We were, anyway.

What was it like, say, running around discotheques with the Stones?

Oh, that was a great period. We were like kings of the jungle then, and we were very close to the Stones. I don't know how close the others were, I spent a lot of time with Brian and Mick, and I admire them. I dug them the first time I saw them in whatever that place is they came from, Richmond Club. I spent a lot of time with them and it was great. We were kings and we were all just at the prime and we all used to just go around London in our cars and meet each other and talk about music with the Animals and Eric and all that. It was really a good time. That

Opposite: Brian Jones with Keith Richard, 1967

was the best period, fame-wise, we didn't get mobbed so much. I don't know, it was like a men's smoking club, just a very good scene.

What was Brian like?

Brian Jones?

Yes.

Well, he was different over the years as he disintegrated. He ended up the kind of guy that you dread he'd come on the phone, you know, because you knew it was trouble. He was really in a lot of pain. But in the early days he was all right, because he was young and confident. He was one of them guys that disintegrated in front of you. And he was all right, and he wasn't sort of brilliant or anything, he was just a nice guy.

What did you feel when he died?

By then I didn't feel anything, really. I just thought, another victim of the drug scene.

What do you think of the Stones today?

I think it's a lot of hype, you know. I like "Honky Tonk Woman" and I think Mick's a joke, with all that fag dancing, I always did. I enjoy him, you know, I'll go and see his films and all probably, like everybody else, but really, I think it's a joke.

Do you see him much now?

No, I never do see him. We saw a bit of each other around when Allen was first coming in. I think Mick got jealous, but I was always very respectful about Mick and the Stones. But he said a lot of sort of tarty things about the Beatles, which I am hurt by, because, you know, I can knock the Beatles, but don't let Mick Jagger knock them. Because I would like to just list what we did and what the Stones did two months after, on every fuckin' album and every fuckin' thing we did. And Mick does exactly the same—he imitates us. And I would like one of you fuckin' underground people to point it out. You know *Satanic Majesties* is *Pepper.* "We Love You," man, it's the most fuckin' bullshit, that's "All You Need Is Love." I resent the implication that the Stones are like revolutionaries and that the Beatles weren't. If the Stones were or are, the Beatles really were, too. They are not in the same class, music-wise or power-wise, never were. I never said anything, I always admired them because I like their funky music and I like their style.

Sgt. Pepper and the critics

YOKO: But you always liked rock and roll.

JOHN: Yeah, I like rock and roll and the direction they took after they got over trying to imitate us. But he's even going to do Apple now. He's going to do the same thing, and if it happens he'll do exactly what we did and be . . . lose all his money. He's obviously so upset by how big the Beatles are compared with him, and he never got over it. And he's now in his old age and he is beginning to knock us, you know, and he keeps knocking because the Beatles . . . like everybody jumped in on the bandwagon to knock Beatles when we split and formed Apple. Mick said "Peace" made money. We didn't make any money from "Peace."

YOKO: We lost money.

When Sgt. Pepper *came out did you know after you had put it together that it was a great album?*

Sgt. Pepper?

Did you feel that while you were making it?

Yeah, yeah, and *Rubber Soul* too, and *Revolver.*

What did you think of the review in the New York Times of Sgt. Pepper?

I don't remember it. Did it pan it?

Yes.

I don't remember. In those days reviews weren't very important because we had it made

"Can't you be without Yoko?"

whatever happened. Nowadays I'm sensitive as shit, and every review counts. But those days we were too big to touch. I don't remember the reviews at all, I never read them. We were so blasé, we never even read the news clippings. I didn't bother with them or read anything about us. It was a bore to read about us. Maybe Brian told us, or somebody told us about it, that it was great or lousy, I don't even remember even hearing about it.

That was the first real anti-Beatles thing in the United States.

Yeah, well, they've been . . . they've been trying to knock us down since we began, including the British press. Always saying, 'What are you going to do when the bubble bursts?' And we told them, privately, etc, that we'd go when *we decided*, not when some fickle public decided. Because we're not a manufactured group; that we are what we are because we know what we're doing. Of course we've made many mistakes, etc, etc. But we knew instinctively that it would end when we decided and not when the ATV decides to take off our series, or anything like that. There was very few things that happened to Beatles that weren't really well thought out by us whether to do it or not, and what reaction, and would it last forever. We had an instinct for it, like somebody wrote.

Why can't you be alone without Yoko?

I can be, but I don't wish to be.

There is no reason on earth why I should be without her. There is nothing more important than our relationship, nothing. And we dig being together all the time. And both of us could survive apart, but what for? I'm not going to sacrifice love, real love, for any fuckin' whore or any friend, or any business, because in the end you're

"Creating is a result of pain"

alone at night. Neither of us want to be and you can't fill the bed with groupies, that doesn't work. I don't want to be a swinger. Like I said in the song, I've been through it all and nothing works better than to have somebody you love hold you.

There was a while in which you hid out in Weybridge where you sat home all the time and did nothing . . .

Well, that's what they say, but I wrote a lot of songs and made some what would be termed 'far out' tapes, which I still have. And I made a lot of movies on 8mm. But at the time I used to think that was not doing anything; I thought if I wasn't doing sort of Beatle work, it wasn't work.

You said at one point you have to write songs that can justify your existence.

I said a lot of things. I write songs because that's the thing I choose to do, you know, and I can't help writing them, that's a fact. And sometimes I feel as though you work . . . I felt as though you worked to justify your existence, but you don't. You work to exist and vice versa, and that's it, really.

You say you write songs because you can't help it.

Yeah, creating is a result of pain, too. I have to put it somewhere and I write songs. But that hiding in Weybridge, I used to think I wasn't working there. I made twenty or thirty movies, on just 8mm stuff, but they are still movies. And many, many hours of tape of different sounds, just not rocking, I suppose you would call them avant-garde. That's how Yoko met me. I'd play . . . I mean there was very few people I could play those tapes to, and I played them to her and then we made "Two Virgins" a few hours later.

How are you going to avoid going overboard on things again?

"Helter Skelter" and Manson

I think I'll be able to control meself . . . control is the wrong word, I just won't get involved in too many things, that's all, I think. I'll just do whatever happens. It's silly to feel guilty that I'm not working, that I'm not doing this or that, it's just stupid. I'm just going to do what I want for meself, for both of us.

What happened to Magic Alex?

I don't know, he's still in London.

Did you all really think that he had these inventions?

I think some of his stuff actually has come true. They just haven't manufactured . . . maybe one of the whole midst is a saleable object. He was just another guy, you know, that comes and goes around people like us. He's all right, but he's cracked. He means well.

You say on your record that "freaks on the phone won't leave me alone, so don't give me that brother, brother . . ."

Because I'm sick of all these aggressive hippies or whatever they are, the Now Generation, sort of being very uptight with me, you know, either on the street or anywhere, or on the phone, demanding my attention as if I owed them something. I'm not their fucking parents, that's what it is. They come to the door with a fucking peace symbol and expect to just sort of march around the house or something like an old Beatle fan. They're under a delusion of awareness by having long hair and that's what I'm sick of. I'm sick of them, they frighten me, a lot of uptight maniacs going around wearing fuckin' peace symbols.

What did you think of Manson and that thing?

I don't know what I thought when it happened, I just think a lot of the things he says are true, that he is a child of the state, made by us, and he took their children in when nobody else would, is what he did. Of course he's cracked, all right.

What about "Helter Skelter"?

Well, he's balmy, he's like any other Beatle kind of fan who reads mysticism into it. I mean we used to have a laugh putting this, that, or the other in, in a light-hearted way. Some intellectual would read us, some symbolic youth generation wants it, but we also took seriously some parts of the role . . . but, I don't know, what's "Helter Skelter" got to do with knifing somebody? I've never listened to the words properly, it was just a noise.

"We used to have a laugh putting this, that or the other in"

Everybody spoke about the playing backwards thing on Abbey Road.

That's bullshit. I just read one about Dylan, too, that he sings . . . I don't believe it, that's bullshit.

The rumor about Paul being dead . . .

We've been through all this before.

About the rumor?

About Paul being dead, I don't know where that started, that's balmy. I don't know, you know as much about it as me.

Were any of those things on the album that they said were on the album?

Name a few.

This whole list of clues . . .

No, that was bullshit. The whole thing was made up. We wouldn't do anything like that. We put in like "tit, tit, tit" in "Girl," and, I don't remember . . . there would be things like a beat missing or something like that to see if anybody noticed. I know we used to have a few things but nothing that could be interpreted like that.

Why do you think people would start rumors, like that whole death thing would happen . . .

People have got nothing better to do than

study Bibles and make myths about it, and study rocks and make stories about how people used to live and all that. You know, it's just something to do for them, they live vicariously.

There is a point at which you decided you would give up your private life, you and Yoko would give up your private life . . .

No, we never decided to give up our private life. We decided that if we were going to do anything like get married, or like this film we are going to make now, that we would dedicate it to peace and the concept of peace. And during that period, because we are what we are, it evolved that somehow we ended up being responsible to produce peace. You know, even in our own heads we would get that way. Peace is still important and my life is dedicated to living, just surviving is what it's about, really, from day to day.

What happened in Denmark, during that peace festival time?

Hamrick was brought over by Tony because he said this was a great doctor and he hadn't mentioned about the flying saucers until he was on his way, almost. But this guy was going to hypnotize us and we would stop smoking.

Yoko: We felt it was very practical.

John: So we thought, great. Tony said it really worked because it worked on him and it had worked. Tony and Melinda stopped smoking. He said it was easy. So he was brought over and this big guy comes in who seemed to be primaling all the time, he was always crying a lot and talking, and then he tried it and it didn't work. He talked like crackers and then he said he would put us back into our past lives. We were game for anything then, you know, so it's like going to a fortune teller and we said all right, do it.

Hamrick and the Flying Saucer

And he was mumbling, pretending to hypnotize us, and we're lying there and he's making up all of these Walt Disney stories about past lives, which we didn't believe, but he was such a nice guy in a way that we didn't want to sort of say, well . . . We were saying it seems a bit strange . . . I was more into it than Yoko, I mean she's not quite as silly as I am. But I was thinking 'you never know, do you?' I had this thing, believe everything until it is disproved. And it came from giving up ciggies and he was going on about how he had been on a space ship, so I said, come on, tell us more.

Yoko: But you were a bit suspicious . . .

John: I was suspicious, but I wouldn't stop the stories coming out. 'Tell how it was,' you know, and then he'd be saying they all think they're . . . there was this Harbinger that I didn't know about, but I heard that Tony and them had been there, Tony had only gone at the end, but they were obviously all insane people. And then these other two came with him, one in purple, the other a magician. He said he was going to put spells . . . really crazy, and we were getting worried by then that it was getting out of hand. But we wondered why this Hamrick, if he was such a higher being, and all of them think they're higher beings, they're still traveling around Europe, and everywhere thinking that they've got messages and it's a shame. And Hamrick said he's been on a flying saucer but we always wondered about somebody so spiritual and ethnic or whatever the shit, why is he so fat? Why can't he get that together? He'd say, 'Well, because I have to get myself in a certain state of being by eating all these ice cream buns to communicate with the Martians.' And the poor old dear and his wife are probably up in Canada now . . . Actually, we went there to see Kyoko. And it was another case of brothers and all that—love me, love my dog.

You said talk is a bad form of communication and that music is a better form of communication.

When did I say that? I don't know, I don't know if it's true or not, it's true one minute and not true the next.

What do you think the future of rock and roll is?

Whatever we make it. If we want to go bullshitting off into intellectualism with rock and roll, we are going to get bullshitting rock intellectualism. If we want real rock and roll, it's up to all of us to create it and stop being hyped by, you know, revolutionary image and long hair. We've got to get over that bit. That's what cutting hair is about. Let's own up now and see who's who, who's doing something about what, and who's making music and who's laying down bullshit. Rock and roll will be whatever we make it.

Why do you think it means so much to people?

Rock and roll?

Yes.

Because it is primitive enough and has no bullshit, really, the best stuff, and it gets through to you its beat. Go to the jungle and they have the rhythm and it goes throughout the world and it's as simple as that. You get the rhythm going, everybody gets into it. I read that Eldridge Cleaver said that blacks gave the middle-class whites back their bodies, you know, put their minds and bodies together through the music. It's something like that, it gets through, to me it got through, it was the only thing to get through to me after all the things that were happening when I was 15. Rock and roll was real, everything else was unreal. And the thing about rock and roll, good rock and roll, whatever good means, is that it's real, and realism gets through to you despite yourself. You recognize something in it which is true, like all true art. Whatever art is, readers, OK? If it's real, it's simple usually, and if it's simple, it's true, something like that. Rock and roll got through to you, finally.

"If somebody attacks, I shrink"

Yoko: I was going to say that classical music was basically 4/4 and then it went into 4/3/2, which is just a waltz rhythm and all of that, but it just went further and further away from the heartbeat. Heartbeat is 4/4. Then rhythm became very decorative, you know, like Schoenberg, Webern. But the point is that it is highly complicated and interesting, and our minds are very much like that, but they lost the heartbeat. I went to see the Beatles' session and in the beginning I thought, 'oh, well.' So I said to John, 'Why do you always use that beat all the time, the same beat, why don't you do something more complex . . . ?'

John: I was doing "Bulldog," it was embarrassing . . .

For yourself or Yoko?

For me, because if somebody starts playing that intellectual on me, I'm going to . . .

Yoko: He's a very shy person.

John: I'm shy, if somebody attacks, I shrink.

Yoko: Intellectual snob that I am . . .

John: She is an intellectual, a supreme intellectual. You see, I really know what I'm talking about when I say 'those fuckin' intellectuals.' They have to have a sort of a math formula happenin' in their head to feel something, they have to go 'this is the result of that, which did this,' 'cause the programming when they were children . . .

Yoko: The best way to explain is 'I can't

lay the piano unless I see a score.'

Early Beatle music

JOHN: Which is insanity . . . that is intel-ectualism. And that is musicianship, that's the chool of music shit, to not be able to make music nless you can read a piece of paper which has othing to do with music.

And you feel the same way about rock and roll now t 30 as you did at 15?

Well, it will never be as new and it will never o what it did to me then, but like "Tutti Frutti" r "Long Tall Sally" is pretty avant-garde. I met n old avant-garde friend of Yoko's in the Village he other day who was talking about one note ike he just discovered that. That's about as far ut as you can get. Even intellectually I can play ames enough for reasons why that music is very mportant and always will be. Like the blues, s opposed to jazz, white middle class good jazz s opposed to the blues . . . the blues is better . .

Because it's simpler?

Because it's real, it's not perverted or thought bout, it's not a concept, it is a chair, not a design or a chair, or a better chair, or a bigger chair, r a chair with leather or with design . . . it is he first chair. It is a chair for sitting on, not hairs for looking at or being appreciated. You it on that music.

How would you describe Beatle music?

Well, it means a lot of things to me. There s not one thing that's Beatle music . . . how can hey . . . I'm part of it, so . . . What is Beatle nusic, "Walrus" or "Penny Lane"? Which? It's hat diverse. "I Want to Hold Your Hand" or Revolution No. 9"?

What do you think it was about "Love Me Do"?

"Love Me Do" is rock and roll, you know, retty funky.

"Love Me Do"

What do you think accounted for the sudden popularity of "Love Me Do"?

"Love Me Do" was never big. It might have made it over here after we'd made it. Remember that America followed much after, 'cause we were local heroes. 'Love Me Do" didn't even make number 40 on the charts in England, it didn't do anything.

What was it about the sound, not particularly "Love Me Do" but any of your first records?

We didn't sound like anybody else, that's all. I mean we didn't sound like the black musicians because we weren't black. And because we were brought up on a different kind of music and atmosphere, and so "Please, Please" and "From Me to You" and all those were our version of the chair. We were building our own chairs, that's all, and they were sort of local chairs.

What were the first devices and tricks that you used?

The first gimmick was the harmonica. There had been "Hey, Baby" and there was a terrible thing called "I Remember You" in England. And I played a lot of harmonica and mouth organ when I was a child. We did those numbers and so we started using it on "Love Me Do" just for arrangements, 'cause we used to work out arrangements and we just used it. And then we stuck it on "Please Please Me" and then we stuck it on "From Me To You" and then it went on and on, it got into a gimmick and then we dropped it, it got embarrassing.

What sort of complexities or embellishment besides harmonica did you start to use?

Well . . . we did that at the Cavern. I was playing harmonica, that was the gimmick in the early days. I don't know what you mean. Musically, on the records what did we do? The first set of tricks was double tracking on the second album. We discovered that, or it was told to us, you can do this, and that really set the ball rolling. We'd double tracked ourselves off the album on the second album. Not really. Apart from that, the first lot we just did as a group, we went in and played and they put it on tape and we went. They remixed it, they did everything to it. I would love to remix some of the early stuff, because it is better than it sounds.

A live album?

Yoko: And I want to cover some, John.

John: Yes, yes. She's going to do Lennon-McCartney albums. You've got to do your old . . . you've got so many albums . . .

Have you ever thought, there's a live album . . .

Hollywood Bowl—it's pretty tatty, it's nice to hear, it'll probably go out one day, I suppose. But we were so nervous, the Hollywood Bowl was just . . . it's all those . . . it was almost like Dean Martin and all those . . . it wasn't like people any more. And we were always nervous, it was like going on the Palladium. But we were there all right . . . there's also Shea Stadium somewhere, too. There's one in Italy apparently that somebody recorded there. But we always did everything 20 times faster than normal.

What did you think of those concerts like the Hollywood Bowl?

It was awful, I hated it. Some of them were good, some of them weren't. I didn't like Hollywood Bowl. If we knew we were being recorded it was death, we were so frightened. I mean 'cause you knew it was always terrible, your voice was always, you could never hear yourself and you knew that they were fuckin' it up on the tape anyway, and there was no bass and they never recorded the drums, you could never hear 'em. The sound . . . those places were built for fuckin' orchestras, not groups. Some of those big gigs

Who is the walrus

were good, but not many of them.

In rereading an interview that you did with Jon Cott, a year or so ago, you said something about "A Ticket to Ride" being a favorite song of yours.

Yeah, I liked it because it was slightly a new sound at the time. It's not my favorite song.

In what way?

Because it was pretty fuckin' heavy for then if you go and look in the charts for what other music people were making. And you hear it now and it doesn't sound too bad, it's one of them. But it'd make me cringe. If you give me the A-track and I remix it, I'll show you what it is really, but you can hear it there. I used to like guitars, I didn't want anything else on the album but guitars and jangling piano, or whatever, and it's all happening. It's a heavy record and the drums are heavy, too. That's why I like it.

In "I Am the Walrus" . . .

That was the B-side of "Hello, Goodbye," can you believe it?

. . . you say in "Glass Onion": "here's another clue for you all . . ."

"The Walrus is Paul." Ray Coleman asked me. At that time I was still in my love cloud with Yoko, I thought well, I'll just say something nice to Paul, that it's all right, you know, and you did a good job over these few years, holding us together. And he was trying to organize the group, and do the music, and be an individual artist, and all that, so I wanted to say something to him, and I did it for that reason, you know, I thought, well, he can have it, I've got Yoko, and thank you, you can have the credit.

Opposite: Lennon and Zappa, Fillmore East, 1971

And now you've decided . . .

I've decided I'm sick of . . . between reading things about Paul is the musician, and George is the philosopher, I wonder where I fit in, what

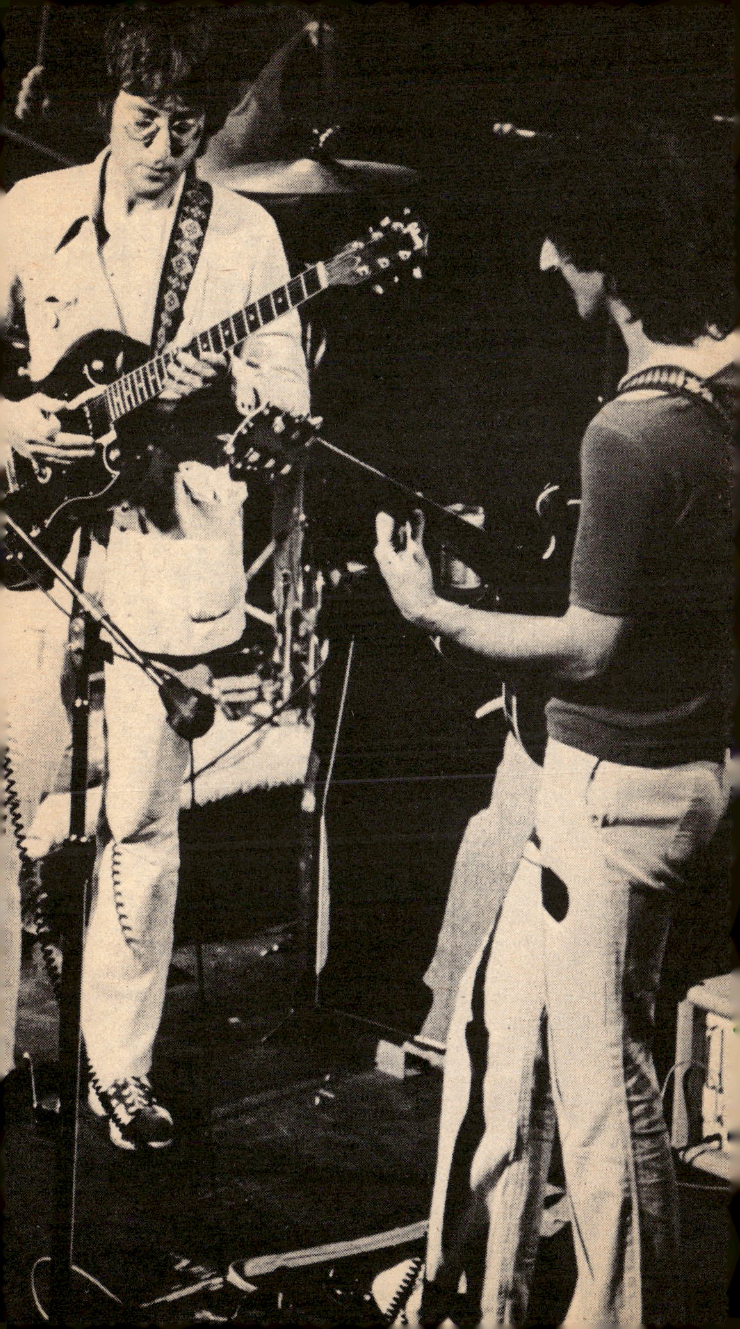

was my contribution? I get hurt, you know, I'm sick of it. So I'd sooner be like Zappa and say, listen you fuckers, this is what I did, and I don't care whether you like my attitude saying it, but that's what I am, you know, I'm a fuckin' artist, and I'm not a fuckin' PR agent, or the product of some other person's imagination. Whether you're the public or whatever, you know, I'm standing by me work, whereas before I would not stand by it. So that's what I'm saying.

I was the Walrus, whatever that means. We saw the movie in LA and the Walrus was a big capitalist that ate all the fuckin' oysters, if you must know, that's what he was. I always had this image of the Walrus in the garden and I loved it, and so I didn't ever check what the Walrus was. I didn't go around saying 'I'm the Walrus, is it something?' But he's a fucking bastard, that's what he turns out to be. But the way it's written, . . . everybody presumes that means something, I mean even I did, so we all just presumed . . . just 'cause I said I am the Walrus that it must mean I am God or something, but it's just poetry. But it became symbolic of me.

What other things are there like the Walrus?

Oh, I don't know, I said hello to Peter Brown in "The Ballad of John and Yoko." It's just a way of thanking them, 'cause I learned from Yoko the way they always dedicate their work, these avant-garde people, to each other, like this is for David Tudor, and this is for that. And they're great for that. In the original, her whole book is dedicated to all these men; I wouldn't let her put it in the real one, but now I understand it a bit, but I thought they were all sort of . . .

Yoko: No, it wasn't anything special . . .

John: No, I know. Like I dedicated an album

to Yoko, but they would . . . "Isolation" for George, or "Isolation" for Jann, just because you were around when we spoke, or something like that. That's nice. They did that to each other, so it's a bit like that, it's . . .

Yoko: With the drop of a hat, they did . . .

John: They were just in the group and they did a lot of that, so I just sort of picked up on it, I suppose, and I'm very sort of full . . . I want people to love me . . . I want to be loved.

What was it like doing "Instant Karma"? . . . that was your first record with Phil.

Recording it? It was great, you know, because I wrote it in the morning on the piano, and I went to the office and I sang it many times and I sang it, and I said, hell, let's do it and we booked the studio, and Phil came in and he said 'How do you want it?' and I said, you know, '1950s' and he said 'Right,' and boom, I did it, in about three goes. He played it back and there it was. The only argument was I said a bit more bass, that's all, and off we went. You see Phil is a real . . . he's great at that, he doesn't fuss about with fuckin' stereo or all the bullshit, just 'does it sound all right? then let's have it.' It doesn't matter whether something's prominent or not prominent; if it sounds good to you as a layman or as a human, take it, don't bother whether this is like that, or the quality of this . . . just take it, and that suits me fine.

What do you think of "Give Peace a Chance"?

I thought it was beautiful.

Did you ever see the Moratorium Day in Washington?

That's what it was for, you know.

Did you see that scene?

I think I heard it, I don't know. I just remember hearing them all sing it . . . I don't know whether it was on the radio or TV. You know,

"Give Peace a Chance"

it was a very big moment for me, that's what the song was about. You see I'm shy and aggressive, so I have great hopes for what I do with my work and I also have great despair that it's all pointless and it's shit. How can you beat Beethoven or Shakespeare, or whatever? I go through all that, and in me secret heart I wanted to write something that would take over "We Shall Overcome." I don't know why. Maybe because that was the one they always sang. I thought why doesn't somebody write one for the people now, you know, that's what my job is, our job is, to write for the people now, the songs that they go and sing on the buses even, and not just love songs. I had the same kind of hope for "Working Class Hero." I know it's a different concept, but I feel as though . . . I think it's a revolutionary song.

In what respect?

It's really . . . just revolutionary. I just think its concept is revolutionary, and I hope it's for workers and not for tarts and fags. I hope it's about what "Give Peace a Chance" was about. But I don't know, on the other hand it might just be ignored. I think it's for the people like me who are working class, whatever, upper or lower, who are supposed to be processed into the middle classes, or in through the machinery, that's all. It's my experience, and I hope it's just a warning to people, "Working Class Hero" . . .

Yoko: Oh, that's a fantastic song.

John: Don't praise it. I'm saying I think it's a revolutionary song, you know, not the song itself, it's a song for the revolution.

Can you deliberately put out a commercial record, do you have a feeling for a number one record?

No. You see, I keep thinking "Mother" is a commercial record, because all the time I was

writing it, it was the one I was singing most, it's the one that seemed to catch on in my head. I'm convinced "Mother" is a commercial record.

I agree.

You agree? Well, thank you, but you said "God" . . .

No I didn't.

No, no, they're all playing "God" . . . oh, "Isolation" . . .

"Mother" is the one I have in my head all the time.

But there's politics in it, too. Politics will prepare the ground for my album, the same as "Oh My Sweet Lord" prepared the ground for George's. I'm not going to get hits just like that, people aren't going to buy my album just because *Rolling Stone* liked it. People have got to be hyped in a way, they've got to have it presented to them in all the best ways that are possible. And if "Love" . . . because I like the song "Love" you know, I like the melody, and the words, and everything, I think it's beautiful, . . . but I'm more of a rocker.

If you don't take them all at once, and you just take "Love," it's a single song, it's a single record. "Mother" is a single. "Love" is a single. "God" could be, so could "Isolation" and "Remember." I write singles, I write them all the same way. But "Mother," you've got to take into account the lyrics, too. If I can capture more sales by singing about love than singing about my mother, I'll do it.

Yoko: Because that would open a door for . . .

John: I'm opening a door for John Lennon, not for music, or for the Beatles or for a movement or for anything. I'm presenting myself to as broad a scope as I can.

There's that side of the market. I'm not going

Amour
Amore
Amor
Love
Liebe

"Love" counterbalances the suspicion of something nasty.

to disregard it, you know, I mean to sell as many albums as I can, and as many records as I possibly can, because I'm an artist who wants everybody to love me and everybody to buy my stuff, you know, and I'll go for that.

The theory of putting out something that's commercial to get people to buy the album, of course, there's no great shakes about that theory, the question is which is most commercial, "Love" or "Mother"?

The thing is "Love" would attract more people because of the message, man. There are many, many people that would not like "Mother," it hurts them. The first thing that happens to you when you get the album is you can't take it, everybody's reacted exactly the same. They think '*fuck*, that's how everybody is.' And the second time they start saying, oh, there's a little . . . you know. So if I laid "Mother" on them, it confirms the suspicion that something nasty is going on with that John Lennon and his broad again. You see, people aren't that hip, students aren't that aware and all that bullshit, they're just like anybody else: 'oh, misery, is that what it's . . . don't tell me, it's really awful . . .'

Yoko: Why is he accusing his mother?

John: Be a good boy, now, John, or, you had a hard time, but me, me and my mother . . . you know, so there's all that to go through. "Love" I wrote it in a spirit of love . . . it's for Yoko, it has all that connotation for me and it's a beautiful melody, and I'm not even known for writing melody.

If it goes, it'll do me good.

Did you write most of the stuff in this album on guitar or piano?

The ones where I play guitar, I wrote on guitar, the ones where I play the piano, I wrote on piano.

What do you think is the difference between a piano

song and a guitar song, what are the differences to you when you write them?

What are your best songs?

Well, I play the piano even worse than I play guitar, so that is a limited pallette, as they call it. So I surprise meself, you know, I have to think in terms of 'go from C to A,' and I'm not quite sure where I am half the time, and when I'm holding a chord, I go 'ding,' on the guitar it's only a sixth or a seventh or something like that, on the piano I don't know what it is. So it's that kind of feel about it. But with the guitar I know such a lot about the guitar, that with the guitar I can be buskin', or if I want to write a sort of, just a rocker, I have to play guitar because I can't play piano well enough to inspire me to rock . . . like that, so that's the difference, really.

What do you think are your best songs that you have written?

Ever?

Ever. What is the best song you have ever written?

The one best song?

Have you ever thought of that?

I don't know. If somebody asked me what is my favorite song, is it "Stardust" or something . . . I can't . . . that kind of decision making I can't do. I always liked "Walrus," "Strawberry Fields," "Help," "In My Life." Those are some favorites, you know.

Why "Help"?

Because I meant it, it's real. The lyric is as good now as it was then. It's no different, you know, and it makes me feel secure to know that I was that sensible, or whatever, not sensible, but aware of myself then. It was just me singing "Help" and I meant it. I don't like the recording that much, the song I like. We did it too fast, to try to be commercial. I like "I Want to Hold Your Hand," we wrote that together, it's a beautiful melody. I might do "I Want to Hold Your Hand" and "Help" again, because I like them, I sing them, they are the kinds of songs I sing.

Why "Strawberry Fields"? Did you think that was real?

Because it's real, yeah. It was real for then, and it's . . . I think it's like talking, you know . . . it's like that Elton John one where he's singing, oh I don't know, he talks to himself, sort of singing, which I thought was nice, which reminded me of that.

Songs like "Girl"?

Yeah, I liked that one.

"Run for Your Life"?

"Run for Your Life" I always hated.

Why?

I don't know, it was one of them I knocked off just to write a song, and it was phoney. But "Girl" is real. There is no such thing as *the* girl, she was a dream, but the words are all right. It's about 'was she taught when she was young that pain would lead to pleasure, did she understand it,' and all that. They're sort of philosophy quotes. It was reasonable, I was thinkin' about it when I wrote it; it wasn't just a song, and it was about that girl, that happened to turn out to be Yoko in the end, but the one that a lot of us were looking for. There's many songs I forget that I do like. I like "Across the Universe" too.

Why?

Because it's one of the best lyrics I've written. In fact, it could be *the* best, I don't know. It's one of the best, it's good poetry, or whatever you call it, without chewin' it, it stands. See, the ones I like are the ones that stand as words without melody, that don't have to have any melody. It's a poem, you know, you could read 'em.

That's your ultimate criterion?

Filming *Let It Be*

No, that's just the ones I happen to like. I like it when . . . I like to read other people's lyrics, too.

So what happened with "Let It Be"?

Well, it was another one like "Magical Mystery Tour," it's hard to say. In a nutshell, Paul wanted to . . . it was time for another Beatle movie, or something, he wanted us to go on the road, or do something. And George and I were going 'mumble . . . we don't want to do the fucker' and all that. He sort of set it up, and there was discussions about where to go and all of that, and I would just tag along, and I had Yoko by then and I didn't even give a shit about nothin'. I was stoned all the time, and I just didn't give a shit, you know, and nobody did. Like in the movie, when I got to do "Across the Universe" Paul yawns and plays boogie. And I merely say 'Anyone want to do a fast one?' That's how I am. So year after year that begins to wear you down. I wanted to re-record "Across the Universe" because the original wasn't very good.

How long did those sessions last?

Oh, fuckin' God knows how long. Paul had this idea that he was going to rehearse us. He's looking for perfection all the time and so he has these ideas that we would rehearse and then make the album. And of course we're lazy fuckers and we've been playing for twenty years, for fuck's sake, we're grown men, we're not going to sit around rehearsin', I'm not, anyway . . . we couldn't get into it. And we put down a few tracks and nobody was in it at all. I don't know, it just was a dreadful, dreadful feeling in Twickenham Studio, and being filmed all the time, you know. I just wanted them to go away. And we'd be there eight in the morning and you couldn't make music at eight in the morning or ten or

Opposite: *Let It Be*

whatever it was, in a strange place with people filming you and colored lights.

How did it end?

The tape ended up like the bootleg version. We let Glyn Johns remix it, we didn't want to know, we just left it to him and said, here, do it. It's the first time since the first album that we didn't have anything to do with it. None of us could be bothered going in, Paul, nobody called anybody about it, and the tapes were left there. And we got an acetate each and we called each other and said what do you think, oh, let it out.

We were going to let it out with a really shitty condition, disgusted, and I didn't care, I thought it was good to let it out and show people what had happened to us, 'this is where we're at now, we can't get it together, we don't play together anymore, you know, leave us alone.' So the bootleg version is what it was like. And everyone was probably thinking, 'well, I'm not going to fuckin' work on it.' There was twenty-nine hours of tape, it was like a movie, just so much tape, twenty takes of everything because we were rehearsing and taking everything. Nobody could face looking at it.

So when Spector came around, you know, 'all right, if you want to work with us, go and do your audition.' And he worked like a pig on it. I mean he'd always wanted to work with the Beatles, and he was given the shittiest load of badly recorded shit with a lousy feeling to it ever, and he made something out of it. He did a great job. When I heard it I didn't puke, I was so relieved after hearing six months of this like black cloud hanging over, that this was going to go out. I thought it would be good to go out, the shitty version, because it would break the Beatles,

LOVE

you know, it would break the myth. That's us, with no trousers on and no glossy paint over the cover and no sort of hope. 'This is what we are like with our trousers off, so would you please end the game now.' But that didn't happen. We ended up doing *Abbey Road* quickly, and putting out something slick to preserve the myth.

Why?

To preserve the myth. I am weak as well as strong, you know, and I wasn't going to fight for *Let It Be* because I really couldn't stand it.

Finally when Let It Be *was going to be released, Paul at that point wanted to release his album?*

Well, I don't quite . . . so many clashes . . . it did come out at the same time, or something, did't it? I think he wanted to show he was the Beatles.

By bringing out McCartney?

I think so.

Were you surprised when you heard it, at what he had done?

Very. I expected just a little more, because if Paul and I aren't sort of disagreeing, I feel weak, I think he must feel strong. That's in an argument. Not that we've had much physical argument, you know, I mean when we're talking . . .

What do you think Paul will think of your album?

I think it'll probably scare him, into doing something decent. And then he'll scare me into doing something decent and I'll scare him . . . like that. I think he's capable of great work, I think he will do it. I wish he wouldn't, you know, I wish nobody would, Dylan or anybody. In me heart of hearts I wish I was the only one in the world . . . But I can't see him doing it twice.

What part did you ever play in the songs that are heavily identified with Paul, like "Yesterday"?

"Yesterday" I had nothing to do with.

"I never went much for the covers"

"Eleanor Rigby"?

"Eleanor Rigby" I wrote a good half of the lyrics or more.

When did Paul show you "Yesterday"?

I don't remember—I really don't remember, it was a long time ago. I think he was . . . I really don't remember, it just sort of appeared.

Who do you think has done the best versions of your stuff?

I can't think of anybody.

Did you hear Ike and Tina Turner doing "Come Together"?

Yeah, I think they did too much of a job on it, I think they could have done it better. They did a better "Honky Tonk Woman."

Ray Charles doing "Yesterday"?

That was quite nice.

And you had Otis doing "Day Tripper," what did you think of that?

I don't think he did a very good job on "Day Tripper."

I never went much for the covers. It doesn't interest me, really. I like people doing them—I've heard some nice versions on "In My Life," I don't know who it was, though [Judy Collins]. Jose Feliciano did "Help" quite nice once. I like people doing it, I get a kick out of it. I think it was interesting that Nina Simone did a sort of answer to "Revolution." That was very good—it was sort of like "Revolution," but not quite. That I sort of enjoyed, somebody who reacted immediately to what I had said.

Who wrote "Nowhere Man"?

Me, me.

Did you write that about anybody in particular?

Probably about myself. I remember I was just going through this paranoia trying to write something and nothing would come out so I just lay

"We were both in each other's pies."

down and tried to not write and then this came out, the whole thing came out in one gulp.

What songs really stick in your mind as being Lennon-McCartney songs?

"I want to Hold Your Hand," "From Me To You," "She Loves You"—I'd have to have the list, there's so many, trillions of 'em. Those are the ones. In a rock band you have to make singles, you have to keep writing them. Plenty more. We both had our fingers in each other's pies.

I remember that the simplicity on the new album was evident on the Beatles double album. It was evident in "She's So Heavy," in fact a reviewer wrote of "She's So Heavy": 'He seems to have lost his talent for lyrics, it's so simple and boring.' "She's So Heavy" was about Yoko. When it gets down to it, like she said, when you're drowning you don't say 'I would be incredibly pleased if someone would have the foresight to notice me drowning and come and help me,' you just *scream*. And in "She's So Heavy" I just sang "I want you, I want you so bad, she's so heavy, I want you," like that. I started simplifying my lyrics then, on the double album.

A song from the Help *album, like "You've Got to Hide Your Love Away"—how did you write that? What were the circumstances? Where were you?*

I was in Kenwood and I would just be songwriting. The period would be for songwriting and so every day I would attempt to write a song and it's one of those that you sort of sing a bit sadly to yourself, "Here I stand, head in hand . . ."

I started thinking about my own emotions—I don't know when exactly it started like "I'm a Loser" or "Hide Your Love Away" or those kind of things—instead of projecting myself into a situation I would try to express what I felt about

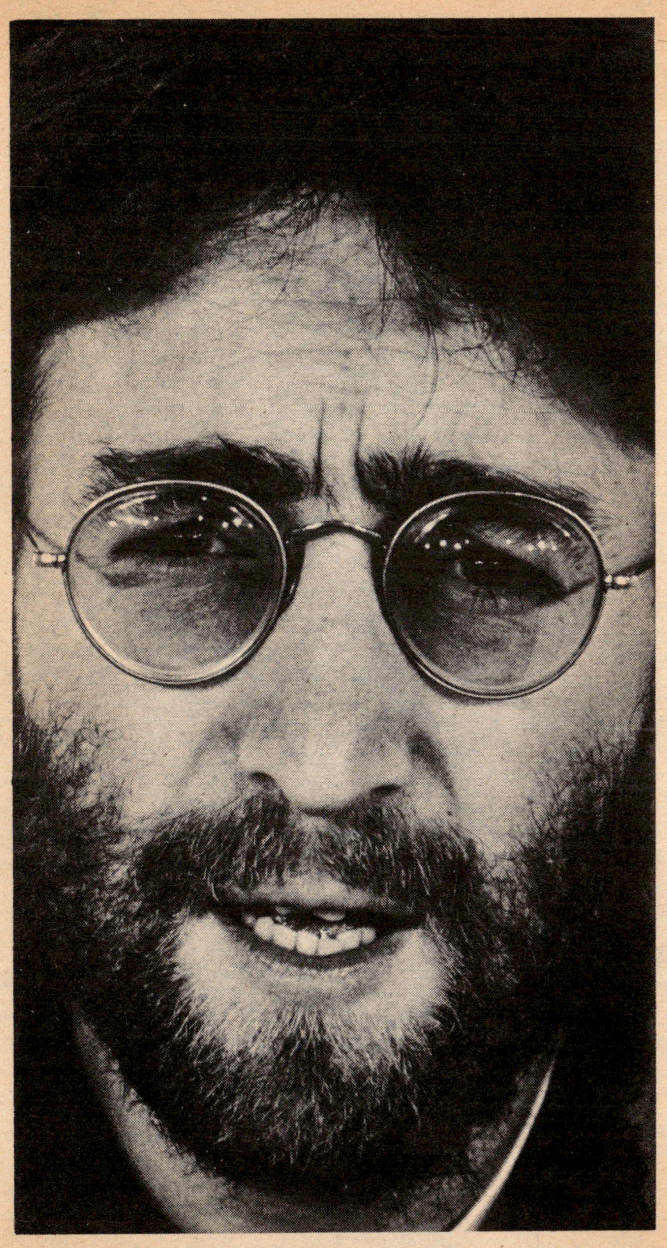

myself which I'd done in me books. I think it was Dylan helped me realize that—not by any discussion or anything but just by hearing his work—I had a sort of professional songwriter's attitude to writing pop songs; he would turn out a certain style of song for a single and we would do a certain style of thing for this and the other thing. I was already a stylized songwriter on the first album. But to express myself I would write *Spaniard in the Works* or *In His Own Write,* the personal stories which were expressive of my personal emotions. I'd have a separate songwriting John Lennon who wrote songs for the sort of meat market, and I didn't consider them—the lyrics or anything—to have any depth at all. They were just a joke. Then I started being me about the songs, not writing them objectively, but subjectively.

What about on Rubber Soul*—"Norwegian Wood"?*

I was trying to write about an affair without letting me wife know I was writing about an affair, so it was very gobbledegook. I was sort of writing from my experiences, girls' flats, things like that.

Where did you write that?

I wrote it at Kenwood.

When did you decide to put a sitar on it?

I think it was at the studio. George had just got the sitar and I said 'Could you play this piece?' We went through many different sort of versions of the song, it was never right and I was getting very angry about it, it wasn't coming out like I said. They said, 'Well just do it how you want to do it' and I said, 'Well, I just want to do it like this.' They let me go and I did the guitar very loudly into the mike and sang it at the same time and then George had the sitar and

I asked him could he play the piece that I'd written, you know, dee diddley dee diddley dee, that bit, and he was not sure whether he could play it yet because he hadn't done much on the sitar but he was willing to have a go, as is his wont, and he learned the bit and dubbed it on after. I think we did it in sections.

You also have a song on that album "In My Life." When did you write that?

I wrote that in Kenwood, I used to write upstairs where I had about ten Brunell tape recorders all linked up, I still have them, I'd mastered them over the period of a year or two—I could never make a rock and roll record but I could make some far out stuff on it. I wrote it upstairs, that was one where I wrote the lyrics first and then sang it. That was usually the case with things like "In My Life" and "Universe" and some of the ones that stand out a bit.

Would you just record yourself and a guitar on a tape and then bring it in to the studio?

I would do that just to get an impression of what it sounded like *sung* and to hear it back for judging it—you never know 'til you hear the song yourself. I would double track the guitar or the voice or something on the tape. I think on "Norwegian Wood" and "In My Life" Paul helped with the middle eight, to give credit where it's due.

From the same period, same time, I never liked "Run For Your Life," because it was a song I just knocked off. It was inspired from—this is a very vague connection—from "Baby Let's Play House." There was a line on it—I used to like specific lines from songs—"I'd rather see you dead, little girl, than to be with another man"—so I wrote it around that but I didn't think it was that important. "Girl" I liked because I was,

"I was pretty heavy on the Church"

in a way, trying to say something or other about Christianity which I was opposed to at the time.

Why Christianity in that song?

Because I was brought up in the church. One of the reviews of *In His Own Write* was that they tried to put me in this satire boom with Peter Cook and those people that came out of Cambridge, saying well he's just satirizing the normal things like the church and the state, which is what I did in *In His Own Write*. Those are the things that you keep satirizing because they're the only things. I was pretty heavy on the church in both books, but it was never picked up although it was obviously there. I was just talking about Christianity in that—a thing like you have to be tortured to attain heaven. I'm only saying that I was talking about 'pain will lead to pleasure' in "Girl" and that was sort of the Catholic Christian concept—be tortured and then it'll be alright, which seems to be a bit true but not in their concept of it. But I didn't believe in that, that you *have* to be tortured to attain anything, it just so happens that you were.

Let me ask you about one on the double album, "Glass Onion." You set out to write a little message to the audience.

Yeah, I was having a laugh because there'd been so much gobbledegook about *Pepper*, play it backwards and you stand on your head and all that. Even now, I just saw Mel Torme on TV the other day saying that "Lucy" was written to promote drugs and so was "A Little Help From My Friends" and none of them were at all—"A Little Help From My Friends" only says get high in it, it's really about a little help from my friends, it's a sincere message. Paul had the line about "little help from my friends," I'm not sure, he had some kind of structure for it and—we wrote it pretty well 50-50 but it was based on his original idea.

Why did you make "Revolution"?

Which one?

Both.

There's three of them.

Starting with the single.

The single. When George and Paul and all of them were on holiday I made "Revolution" which is on the LP, and "Revolution No. 9" I wanted to put it out as a single but they said it wasn't good enough. I had it all prepared and they came by and they said it wasn't good enough and we put out what, "Hello, Goodbye" or some shit like that. No, we put out "Hey Jude," which was worthy, I'm sorry. But we could have had both, you know.

I wanted to put out what I felt about revolution, I thought it was about time we fuckin' spoke about it, the same as I thought it was about time we stopped not answering about the Vietnamese war. On tour with Brian, when we had to tell him we're going to talk about the war this time and we're not going to just waffle, and I wanted to say what I thought about revolution. I had been thinking about it up in the hills in India and I still had this, you know, God will save us feeling about it, it's going to be all right. But even now I'm saying 'Hold on John, it's going to be all right,' otherwise I won't hold on. But that's why I did it, I wanted to talk, I wanted to say my piece about revolution. I wanted to tell you, or whoever listens, and communicate, to say this is what I say.

On one version I said about violence, in or out, I think, because I don't fancy a violent revolution happening all over. I don't want to die, you know. I began to think what else can happen,

"Number Nine" was just a joke

you know, it seems inevitable. And the "Revolution No. 9" was an unconscious picture of what I actually think will happen when it happens. That was just like a drawing of revolution. All the thing was made with loops, I had about thirty loops going, I fed them on to one basic track and one loop . . . I was getting like classical tapes going upstairs and chopping it and making it backwards and things like that to get the sound effects and one thing was an engineer's testing tape where they come on talking and I would say "this is EMI, test series number nine" and I would just cut up whatever he said and I'd number nine it; and nine, turned out to be my birthday and my luck number and everything. I didn't realize it, it was just so funny, the voice saying "number nine" it was like a joke, bringing number nine in it all the time, that's all it was.

Yoko: It turns out to be the highest number, you know, one, two, etc, up to nine.

John: There are many symbolic things about it, but it just happened. It was an engineer's tape and I was just using all the bits, like to make a montage. But I really wanted that released. So that's my feeling. And I know the Chairman Mao bit. I always feel a bit strange about because I thought that if they are going to get hurt, you know, the idea was, don't aggravate the pig by waving the thing that aggravates, by waving the red flag in his face. I really thought that love would save us all. But now I'm wearing a Chairman Mao badge, that's where it's at. I'm not . . . I'm just beginning to think he's doing a good job, he seems to be. I would never know until I went to China. I'm not going to be like that, I was just always interested enough to sing about him, but I just wondered what the kids were doing that were actually Maoists. I wondered

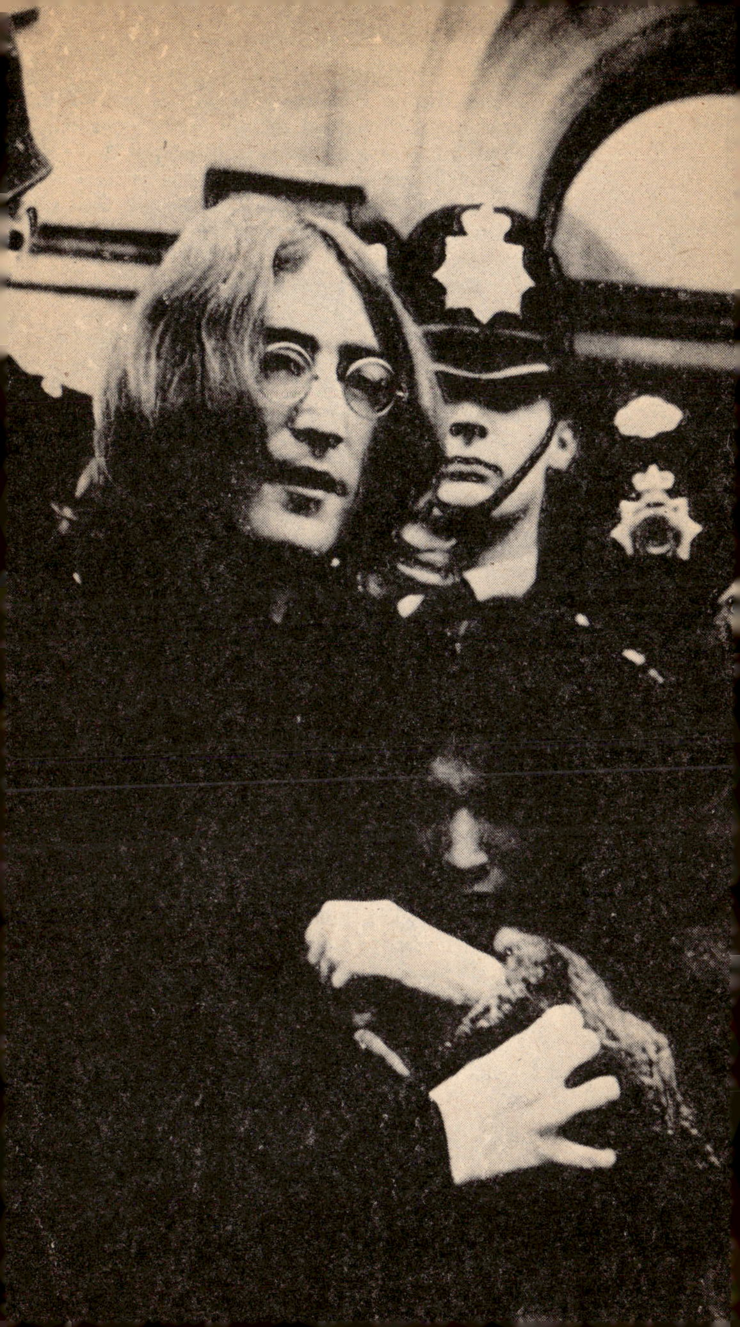

what their motive was or what was really going on, and I thought if they wanted revolution, if they really wanted to be subtle, well that's the point of saying, 'Well, I'm a Maoist and why don't you shoot me down.' I thought that was not a very clever way of getting what they wanted.

You don't really believe that we are headed for a violent revolution?

I don't know. I've got no more conception than you, I can't see . . . eventually it will happen, like it will happen . . . it has to happen, what else can happen? It might happen now, or it might happen in 50 or 100 years, but—

Having a violent revolution now would really just be the end of the world.

Not necessarily, they say that every time, but I don't really believe it, and if it is, OK. I'm back to where I was when I was 17; at 17 I used to think I wish a fuckin' earthquake or revolution would happen so that I could go out and steal and do what the blacks are doing now. If I was black I'd be all for it, if I were 17 I'd be all for it because what've you got to lose? And now I've got nothing to lose. I don't want to die, and I don't want to be hurt physically, but fuck, if they blow the world up, fuck, we're all out of our pain then, forget it! No more problems.

You're saying "Hold on World" . . .

Yeah, I'm saying "Hold on John" too because I don't want to die. I'm a coward . . . well, I'm not a coward, but I don't want to die, I don't want to be hurt and please don't hit me.

So you don't mean by holding on that it will be all right . . .

It's only going to be all right . . . now, at this moment it's all right . . . the thing that we forget about the acid is to live now, this moment. Hold

"Lucy in the Sky" and "Sgt. Pepper"

on now, we might have a cup of tea, we might get a moment's happiness any minute now. So that's what it's all about, just moment by moment. That's how we're living now, but really living like that and cherishing each day, and dreading it too. It might be your last, I mean it sounds funny, but you might get run over by a car and all that. I'm really beginning to cherish it when I'm cherishing it.

I like the philosophy of hold on, 'cause there's really nothing else to do.

Yeah, just hold on, day to day.

"Happiness Is a Warm Gun" is a nice song.

Oh, I like that one of my best, I had forgotten about that. Oh, I love it. I think it's a beautiful song. I like all the different things that are happening in it. Like "God," I had put together some three sections of different songs, it was meant to be—it seemed to run through all the different kinds of rock music.

It wasn't about "H" at all. "Lucy in the Sky with Diamonds" which I swear to God, or swear to Mao, or to anybody you like, I had no idea spelled LSD—and "Happiness"—George Martin had a book on guns which he had told me about—I can't remember—or I think he showed me a cover of a magazine that said "Happiness Is A Warm Gun." It was a gun magazine, that's it: I read it, thought it was a fantastic, insane thing to say. A warm gun means that you just shot something.

When did you realize that those were the initials of "Lucy in the Sky with Diamonds"?

Only after I read it or somebody told me, like you coming up. I didn't even see it on the label. I didn't look at the initials. I don't look—I mean I never play things backwards. I listened to it as I made it. It's like there will be things on this

"A Day In The Life" was real

one, if you fiddle about with it. I don't know what they are. Every time after that though I would look at the titles to see what it said, and usually they never said anything.

You said to me Sgt. Pepper *is the one. That was the album?*

Well, it was a peak. Paul and I were definitely working together, especially on "A Day In The Life" that was a real . . . The way we wrote a lot of the time: you'd write the good bit, the part that was easy, like "I read the news today" or whatever it was, then when you got stuck or whenever it got hard, instead of carrying on, you just drop it; then we would meet each other, and I would sing half, and he would be inspired to write the next bit and vice versa. He was a bit shy about it because I think he thought it's already a good song. Sometimes we wouldn't let each other interfere with a song either, because you tend to be a bit lax with someone else's stuff, you experiment a bit. So we were doing it in his room with the piano. He said "Should we do this?" "Yeah, let's do that."

I keep saying that I always preferred the double album, because *my* music is better on the double album; I don't care about the whole concept of *Pepper*, it might be better, but the music was better for me on the double album, because I'm being myself on it. I think it's as simple as the new album, like "I'm So Tired" is just the guitar. I felt more at ease with that than the production. I don't like production so much. But *Pepper* was a peak all right.

Yoko: People think that's the peak and I'm just so amazed . . . John's done all that Beatle stuff. But this new album of John's is a real peak, that's higher than any other thing he has done.

John: Thank you, dear.

LOVE

"Sergeant Lennon"

Do you think it is?

Yeah, sure. I think it's "Sergeant Lennon." I don't really know how it will sink in, where it will lie, in the spectrum of rock and roll and the generation and all the rest of it, but I know what it is. It's something else, it's another door.

Yoko: That you don't even know yet or realize it.

John: I'm sneakingly aware of it, but not fully, until it is all over like anyone else. We didn't really know what *Pepper* was going to do or what anything was going to do. I had a feeling, but, I don't know whether it's going to settle down in a minority position. The new album could do that because in one way it's terribly uncommercial, it's so miserable in a way and heavy; but it's reality, and I'm not going to veer away from it for anything.

Yoko: I was thinking that Tom Jones is like medium without message, but John's stuff is like the *message* is the medium; it's the message. He didn't need any decorative sound, or decorativeness about it. That is why in some songs it seems that the accompaniment is simple but it's like an urgent message, I feel.

John: Thank you and good night.

How did you get in touch with Allen Klein?

I got various messages through various people that 'Allen Klein would like to talk to you.' Really, it was Mick who got us together. I mean I knew who he was. I didn't want to talk. I had heard about him over the years; the first time I heard about him was that he said one day he would have the Beatles, and this was when Brian was with us. He had offered Brian this good deal, which in retrospect was something Brian should have done. This was years ago. I had heard about all these dreadful rumors about him but I could

Opposite: John and Yoko with Allen Klein (top) and Jonas Mekas (bottom)

Meeting Allen Klein

never coordinate it with the fact that the Stones seemed to be going on and on with him and nobody ever said a word. Mick's not the type to just clam up, so I started thinking he must be all right.

But still, when I heard he wanted to see me, I got nervous, because 'some business man wants to see me, it's going to be business and business makes me nervous.' Finally I got a message from Mick—Allen had really set up the whole deal you know, Mick and us nearly went into Apple together a few years back and we had big meetings and discussions about the studios and all of that, but it never happened—and Allen would have come in that way. That was after Brian died, but it didn't happen. All these approaches were coming from all over the place, and then I met him at the Rock and Roll Circus [the TV film] which has never been seen, with John and Yoko performing together for the first time with a crazy violinist and Keith on bass and all that—always regret that—and I met him there. I didn't know what to make of him; we just shook hands and then . . . Yoko, what happened next?

Yoko: Then one day we finally decided to meet him, you remember . . .

John: I don't know, we just decided to meet him. Did we call him or did we accept *his* call? He called me once, but I never accepted it; I never accepted the call at the house; I think in Kenwood once he called, and I didn't take it, I was too nervous.

I don't like talking to strangers as it is—strangers want to talk about reality, or something else—so I didn't accept the call. Then finally did we accept the call or did I put a call through? He'll tell you.

Do you know he knows the lyrics to every

Opposite: Lennon, Eric Clapton, Keith Richard and Mitch Mitchell at the Rock 'n Roll Circus

CIRCUS

Everyone was nervous

fuckin' song you could ever imagine from the Twenties on? I was with him last night eating, and I was just singing a few things—Yoko thinks I know every song, I know millions of songs—I'm like a juke box, thousands upon millions. G chords and so on—but Allen not only knows it, but he knows every fuckin' word, even the chorus. He's got a memory like *that*, so ask him. But then we met and it was very traumatic.

In what way?

We are both very nervous. He was nervous as shit, and I was nervous as shit, and Yoko was nervous. We met at the Dorchester, we went up to his room, and we just went in you know.

He was sitting there all nervous. He was all alone, he didn't have any of his helpers around, because he didn't want to do anything like that. But he was very nervous, you could see it in his face. When I saw that I felt better. We talked to him a few hours, and we decided that night, he was it!

What made you decide that?

He not only knew my work, and the lyrics that I had written but he also understood them, and from *way* back. That was it. If he knew what I was saying and followed my work, then that was pretty damn good, because it's hard to see me, John Lennon, amongst that. He talked sense about what had happened. He just said what was going on, and I just knew.

He is a very intelligent guy; he told me what was happening with the Beatles, and my relationship with Paul and George and Ringo. He knew every damn thing about us, the same as he knows everything about the Stones. He's a fuckin' sharp man.

There are things he doesn't know, but when it comes to that kind of business, he knows. And anybody that knew me that well—without having met me—had to be a guy I could let look after me.

"I did have the co-operation of a good mind like Paul's"

So I wrote to Sir Joe Lockwood that night. We were so pleased, I didn't care what the others might say. I told Allen, 'You can handle *me*.'

Yoko had become my advisor so that I wouldn't go into Maharishi's anymore. It was Derek and Yoko and I interviewing people coming in to take over Apple when we were running it at Wigmore Street, and Yoko would sit behind me and I'd play me games and she would tell me what they were doing when I blinked, and how they were in her opinion, because she wasn't as stupid or emotional as me. And I've never had that except when the Beatles were against the world I did have the cooperation of a good mind like Paul's. It was us against them.

So you wrote Lockwood?

So I wrote Lockwood saying: 'Dear Sir Joe: From now on Allen Klein handles all my stuff,' Allen has it framed somewhere. I posted it that night and Allen couldn't believe it. He was so excited—'At last, at last!' He was trying not to push, and I was just saying 'You can handle me, and I'll tell the others you seem all right and you can come and meet George and everything, and Paul and all of them.'

I had to present a case to them, and Allen had to talk to them himself. And of course, I promoted him in the fashion in which you will see me promoting or talking about something. I was enthusiastic about him and I was relieved because I had met a lot of people including Lord Beeching who was one of the top people in Britain and all that. Paul had told me, 'Go and see Lord Beeching' so I went. I mean I'm a good boy, man, and I saw Lord Beeching and he was no help at all. I mean, he was all right. Paul was in America getting Eastman and I was interviewing all these so-called top people, and they were animals. Allen was a human being, the same as Brian was a human being. It was the same thing with Brian in the early days, it was an assessment; I make a lot of mistakes character-wise, but now and then I make a good one and Allen is one, Yoko is one and Brian was one. I am closer to him than to anybody else, outside of Yoko.

How did the rest of them react?

I don't remember. They were nervous like me, because this terrible man who had got the Rolling Stones, and said that he was going to get the Beatles years ago—you don't know *what's* going on. I can't remember. I don't know what we did next . . .

Yoko: So somebody said, please, let's see Allen and Eastman together, and see how it is.

John: Right. But what did I say to George then, did I ring them or something? I suppose I rung them.

Yoko: We were going to Apple all the time so we met George there.

John: What did I say? 'This is Allen Klein, we met him last night.' I just sort of said he was OK, and you should meet and all that.

[*Paul meantime had met and married American photographer Linda Eastman, whose father Lee and brother John were music business lawyers who also wanted to 'manage' the Beatle affairs.*]

Then we got Paul. John Eastman had already been in, in fact, we almost signed ourselves over to the Eastmans at one time, because when Paul presented me with John Eastman, I thought well . . . when you're not presented with a real alternative, you take whatever is going. I would say

(continued)

'yes,' like I said 'Yes, let's do *Let It Be.* I have nothing to produce so I will go along,' and we almost went away with Eastman. But then Eastman made the mistake of sending his son over and not coming over himself, to look after the Beatles, playing it a bit cool.

Finally, when we got near the point when Allen came in, the Eastmans panicked; yet I was still open. I liked Allen but I would have taken Eastman if he would have turned out something other than what he was.

We arranged to see Eastman and Klein together in a hotel where one of them was staying. For the four Beatles and Yoko to go and see them both. We hadn't been in there more than a few minutes when Lee Eastman was having something like an epileptic fit, and screaming at Allen, that he was 'the lowest scum on earth,' and calling him all sorts of names. Allen was sitting there, taking it, you know, just takin' it. Eastman was abusing him with class snobbery. What Eastman didn't know then is that Neil had been in New York and found out that Lee Eastman's real name was Lee Epstein! That's the kind of people they are. But Paul fell for that bullshit, because Eastman's got Picassos on the wall and because he's got some sort of East Coast suit; form and not substance. We were all still not sure and they brought in this fella, and he had a fuckin' fit. We had thought it was one in a million but that was enough for me, soon as he started nailing Klein on his taste. Paul was getting in little digs about Allen's dress. I mean you just go and look at Paul's dress, or at his father, or anything—who the fuck does he think he is? Him talking about dress!

Man, so that was it, and we said, 'fuck it!' I wouldn't let Eastman near me; I wouldn't let

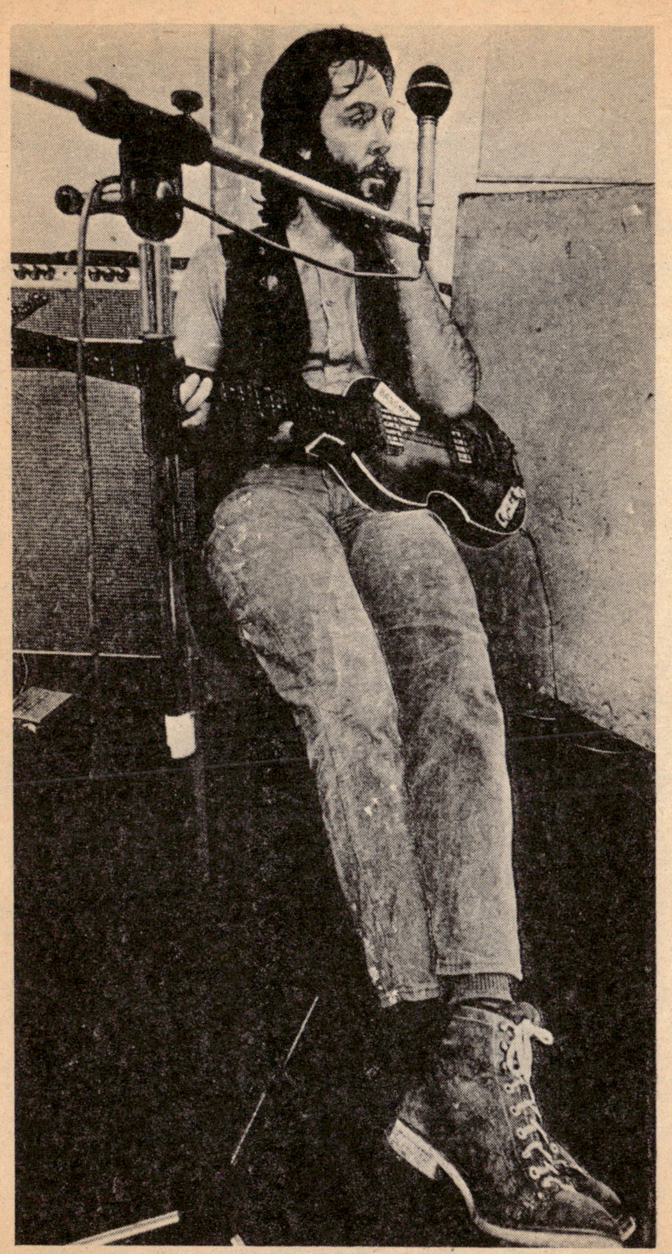

"Its happening to me"

a fuckin' animal like that who has a mind like that near me. Who despises me, too, despises me because of what I am and what I look like.

You know, these people like Eastman and Dick James and people like that, think that I'm a idiot. They really can't see me; they think I'm some kind of guy who got struck lucky, a pal of Paul's or something. They're so fuckin' stupid they don't know.

The reason Allen knew was because he knew who I was. He wasn't going on what a pretty face I've got. Eastman blew it, and then he went on to do it *again.* Where did he do it? Next time he did it was in the Apple office. He kept coming to me, trying to hold his madness down, this insanity that kept coming out. He was coming up to me saying 'I can't tell you how much I admire you.' Gortikov [the former chairman of Capitol Records] does that too; you know them, full of praise, like 'I can't tell you how much I've admired your work, John.'

And I'm just watchin' this and I'm thinkin' 'it's happening to me,' and 'thank you very much,' and all that. [To Yoko:] What was the second fit, because I want this out. What was the second time he blew it?

Yoko: In Apple or something.

John: He did it in front of everybody. This was supposed to be the guy who was taking over the multi-million-dollar corporation, and it was going to be slick. Paul was sort of intimating that Allen's business offices on Broadway were not nice enough as if that were any fuckin' difference! Eastman was in the good section of town. 'Oh, boy, man, that's where it's at!' And Eastman's office has got class! I don't care if this is fuckin' red, white and blue, I don't care what Allen dresses like, he's a human being, man.

So you said 'no' to Eastman, and what did Paul do?

Factional quarrels

The more we said 'no,' the more he said 'yes.' Eastman went mad and shouted and all that. I didn't know what Paul was thinking when he was in the room; I mean, his heart must have sunk.

Yoko: They didn't even want to come to a meeting with Allen.

John: Eastman at first refused to meet Allen. He said 'I will not meet such a low rat.' What the fuck had Klein done? He'd never done a fuckin' thing—he'd been cleared of all this income tax shit—and even if he hadn't, what the fuck, how dare all these fuckin' wolves and sharks call him down for being what he is. How dare they insult anybody like that?

They refused to meet him. I said I don't talk to anybody unless I come along with Allen. They said 'Come on, John, I want to meet you alone,' and I said 'I don't see any of you, unless Allen's with me.'

Yoko: But the thing is that finally when they met, they invited Allen to the Harvard Club. Can you imagine that? Just to show, you know . . .

John: When Eastman was finally signing the Northern Songs deal, God knows what it was, I had to jump over a fence to get Paul's signature for something which finally secured us our position, and then also Eastman lost his temper. He really started insulting me then. Eastman, he knew the game was over. This was in London: three of us had to go there to get his final approval on Paul's signature, which we got. He's initialing all these things just to slow us down, like an immigration officer, really putting us through it. I'm sitting there, waiting, and we're thinking, 'sign it you fuckin' idiot, and let's get

"Don't call my husband stupid"

out,' but he starts insulting me; Yoko said to him 'Will you please stop insulting my husband.' She was saying 'Don't call my husband stupid.' I wasn't saying anything but 'Sign it and give me the signature, just put your initials on it, Epstein,' I was thinking let's get out of here, and we'll wrap you up, and that's what we did.

You can't believe it, man, epileptic fits, and they expected to run the company. Allen even offered to let John Eastman be the lawyer on the deals we were making with Northern Songs. But they were screwing everything Allen did by putting on an argument. It fucked that Northern Songs deal and all that, but we still came out with all the money. Whatever they could do they did but in the end they couldn't out-maneuver him. Klein was the only one who knew exactly what was going on. He not only knew our characters, and what the relationship between the group was, but he also knows his business, he knows who's who in the group, what you have to do to get things done, and he knew about every fuckin' contract and paper we ever had. He understood. Eastman was just making judgments and saying things to Paul based on something that he had never seen. It was a wipe-out, you can't imagine. The real story will come out, because Allen knows every detail and he remembers everything we've said.

Yoko: The first approach was, well . . . he knew I went to Sarah Lawrence. He was saying 'Kafkaesque' and all of that, and talking in a very 'in' way; 'we're middle-class, aren't we?'

But the point is that the Eastman family doesn't know John's a drop-out—I was sick and tired of that middle-class thing and I married a 'working class hero.' And if he is a true aristocrat, he is not going to invite Allen to the Har-

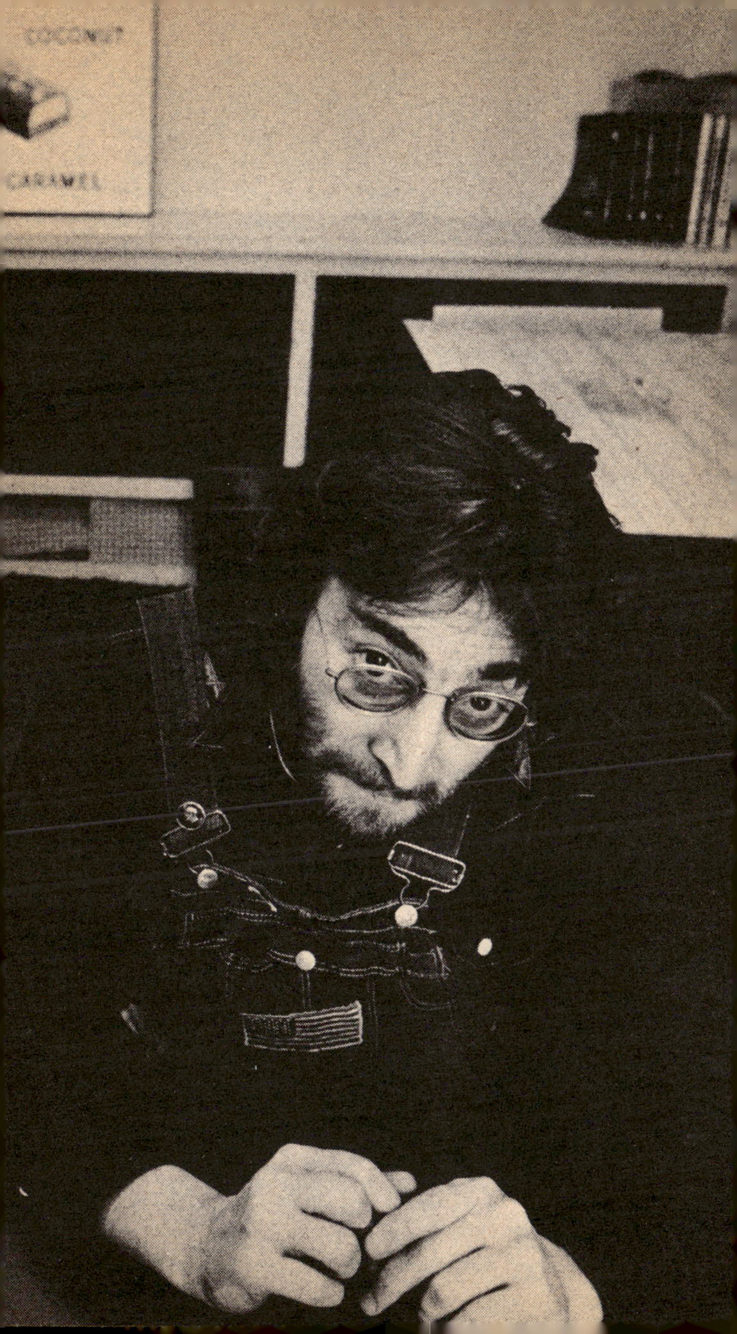
COCONUT
CARAMEL

Beatles business chaos

vard Club, but would make sure that he invites Allen to somewhere Allen would enjoy.

So what was going down with Paul then?

Paul was getting more and more uptight until Paul wouldn't speak to us. He told us 'You speak to my lawyer.'

When did you first start having unpleasant words with Paul?

We never had unpleasant words. It never got to a talking thing, you see, it just got that Paul would say 'Speak to my lawyer, I don't want to speak about business anymore' which meant, 'I'm going to drag my feet and try and fuck you.'

When the whole Northern thing was going on, we tried to save our fuckin' stuff [the publishing rights to most of the Lennon/McCartney songs] and he was playing hard to get, like a fuckin' chick, because *he* hadn't thought of it. It was a pure ego game, and I got into the ego thing, of course, but I was really fighting for our fuckin' business, and what I believed was our money. It wasn't just because I'd found Allen. I would have dropped Allen if Eastman had been something; but he was an animal, a fuckin' stupid middle-class pig, and thought he could con me with fuckin' talking about Kafka, and shit, and Picasso and DeKooning, for Christ's sake, and I shit on the fuckin' lot of them.

I don't even know who the fuck they are; I just know that it's something that somebody has got hung up on the wall that he thinks is an investment.

What was the state of the Beatles' business at that point?

Chaos! Exactly what I've said in the *Rolling Stone*, wasn't it — it all happens in the *Rolling Stone*!

Steve Maltz, I think; Allen said I must have

How much money do you have now?

gotten it from Steve Maltz, this accountant we had had, a young guy, who just sent me a letter one day saying, 'You're in chaos, you're losing money, there is so much a week going out of Apple.'

People were robbing us and living on us to the tune of . . . 18 or 20 thousand pounds a week was rolling out of Apple and nobody was doing anything about it. All our buddies that worked for us for fifty years, were all just living and drinking and eating like fuckin' Rome, and I suddenly realized it and—I said to you—'we're losing money at such a rate that we would have been broke, really broke.'

We didn't have anything in the bank really, none of us did. Paul and I could have probably floated, but we were sinking fast. It was just hell, and it had to stop. When Allen heard me say that—he read it in *Rolling Stone*—he came over right away. As soon as he realized that I knew what was going on, he thought to himself, 'Now I can get through.' Until somebody knows that they are on shit street, how can somebody come and get in . . . it's just like somebody coming up to me *now* and saying 'I want to help you with the business.' I would say 'I've got somebody,' or 'I'm doing all right, Jack . . .' As soon as Allen realized that *I* realized all that was going on, he came over.

How much money do you have now?

I'm not telling. Lots more than I ever had before. Allen has got me more real money in the bank than I've ever had in the whole period and I've got money that I earned for eight or ten years of my fuckin' life, instead of all the Dick James Music Company having it.

How much were you making in that period?

I don't know, I just know it was millions. Brian

Paul kiboshes Ringo

was not a good businessman. He had a flair for presenting things, he was more theatrical than business. He was hyped a lot. He was advised by a gang of crooks, really. That's what went on, and the battle is still going on for the Beatles' rights. The latest one is the Lew Grade thing. If you read Cashbox you'll see what's happening—we've put in a claim to Lew Grade for five million pounds [$12,000,000], in unpaid royalties. They have been underpaying us for years. Dick James—the whole lot of them—sold us out. They still think we're like Tommy Steele or some fuckin' product. None of them realized—simply because of *A Hard Day's Night*—we had to wake up one day, and we were not the same as the last generation of stars or whatever they were called.

How did Paul get down to telling Ringo he was going to get him someday?

It was Paul's new album and he wanted to put it out at the same time *Let It Be* was scheduled to come out. We weren't against him putting an album out, I mean I'd done it, and I didn't think it was any different. Mine happened to be Toronto, because that happened to happen. If I hadn't gone to Toronto, I would have made an album, probably. I was half hoping I would make single after single until there was enough for an album *that* way, because I'm lazy.

We didn't want to put out *Let It Be* and Paul's at the same time. It would have killed the sales. In the old days we used to watch it: if the Stones were coming out . . . we would ask Brian, 'who is coming out?' and he would tell us who's coming out. We could always beat everyone, but what is the point of losing sales? There has to be timing. Mick timed it. We never came out together, we're not idiots. With Elvis, we miss every one;

"I'm not going to record with another egomaniac"

I would miss Tom Jones, anybody, now. I don't want to fight on the charts, I want to get in when the going is good. It would have killed—Paul's was just an ego game—it would have killed *Let It Be.*

We asked Ringo to go and talk to him because Ringo—the real fighting had been going on between me and Paul, because of Eastman and Klein, and we were on the opposite ends of our bats—Ringo had not taken sides, or anything like that, and he had been straight about it, and we thought that Ringo would be able to talk fairly, to Paul—I mean if Ringo agreed that it was unfair, then it was unfair. (At one time Paul wanted a fuckin' extra vote on a voting trust, but that was the same as like the four of us at a table, except that Paul has two votes. I mean, Eastman—something was going on . . . Paul thought he was the fuckin' Beatles, and he never fucking was, never . . . none of us were the fucking Beatles, four of us were.) Ringo went and asked him and he attacked Ringo and he started threatening him and everything, and that was the kibosh for Ringo. What the situation is now, I don't know.

Allen says that you are all going to get together in a few months.

I think that we have to have a meeting shortly, because we are all—we all agreed to meet sometime in February, I think, to see where we are at. Financially, it's business, or whatever.

Do you think you will record together again?

I record with Yoko, but I'm not going to record with another egomaniac. There is only room for one on an album nowadays. There is no point, there is just no point at all. There was a reason to do it at one time, but there is no reason to do it anymore.

Opposite: Ringo in Los Angeles

How the Beatles began

I had a group, I was the singer and the leader; I met Paul and I made a decision whether to—and he made a decision, too—have him in the group: was it better to have a guy who was better than the people I had in, obviously, or not? To make the group stronger or to let me be stronger? That decision was to let Paul in and make the group stronger.

Well, from that, Paul introduced me to George, and Paul and I had to make the decision, or I had to make the decision, whether to let George in. I listened to George play, and I said 'play "Raunchy"' or whatever the old story is, and I let him in. I said 'OK, you come in'; that was the three of us then. Then the rest of the group was thrown out gradually. It just happened like that, instead of going for the individual thing, we went for the strongest format, and for equals.

George is ten years younger than me, or some shit like that. I couldn't be bothered with him when he first came around. He used to follow me around like a bloody kid, hanging around all the time, I couldn't be bothered. He was a kid who played guitar, and he was a friend of Paul's which made it all easier. It took me years to come around to him, to start considering him as an equal or anything.

We had all sorts of different drummers all the time, because people who owned drum kits were few and far between; it was an expensive item. They were usually idiots. Then we got Pete Best, because we needed a drummer to go to Hamburg the next day. We passed the audition on our own with a stray drummer. There are other myths about Pete Best was the Beatles and Stuart Sutcliffe's mother is writing in England that *he* was the Beatles.

"I don't believe in Beatles"

Are you the Beatles?

No, I'm not the Beatles. I'm me. Paul isn't the Beatles. Brian Epstein wasn't the Beatles, neither is Dick James. The Beatles are the Beatles. Separately, they are separate. George was a separate individual singer, with his own group as well, before he came in with us, the Rebel Rousers. Nobody is the Beatles. How could they be? We all had our roles to play.

You say on the record, "I don't believe in the Beatles."

Yeah. I don't believe in the Beatles, that's all. I don't believe in the Beatles myth. "I don't believe in the Beatles"—there is no other way of saying it, is there? I don't believe in them whatever they were supposed to be in everybody's head, including our own heads for a period. It was a dream. I don't believe in the dream anymore.

I made my mind up not to talk about all that shit, I'm sick of it, you know. I would like to talk about the album, I was going to say to you 'Look, I don't want to talk about all that about the Beatles splitting up because it not only hurts me, and it always ends up looking like I'm blabbing off and attacking people.' I don't want it.

How would you assess George's talents?

I don't want to assess him. George has not done his best work yet. His talents have developed over the years and he was working with two fucking brilliant songwriters, and he learned a lot from us. I wouldn't have minded being George, the invisible man, and learning what he learned. Maybe it was hard for him sometimes, because Paul and I are such egomaniacs, but that's the game.

I'm interested in concepts and philosophies. I am not interested in wallpaper, which most music is.

What music do you listen to today?

Current fave listening

If you want the record bit, since I've been listening to the radio here, I like a few things by Neil Young. There are some really good sounds, but, then there is usually no follow-through. There will be a section of fantastic sound come over the radio, then you wait for the conclusion, or the concept or something to finish it off, but nothing happens except it just goes on to a jam session or whatever.

You've had a chance to listen to FM radio in New York. What have you heard?

Yeah. "My Sweet Lord." Every time I put the radio on it's "oh my Lord"—I'm beginning to think there must be a God! I knew there wasn't when "Hare Krishna" never made it on the polls with their own record, that really got me suspicious. We used to say to them, 'You might get number one' and they'd say, 'Higher than that.'

What do we hear? It's interesting to hear Van Morrison. He seems to be doing nice stuff—sort of 1960s black music—he is one of them that became an American like Eric Burdon. I just never have time for a whole album. I only heard Neil Young twice—you can pick him out a mile away, the whole style. He writes some nice songs. I'm not stuck on Sweet Baby [James Taylor]—I'm getting to like him more hearing him on the radio, but I was never struck by his stuff. I like Creedence Clearwater. They make beautiful Clearwater music—they make good rock and roll music. You see it's difficult when you ask me what I like, there's lots of stuff I've heard that I think is fantastic on the radio here, but I haven't caught who they are half the time.

I'm interested in things with more of a worldwide . . . I'm interested in, what's it called, something that means something for everyone, not just

Trying to be Shakespeare

for a few kids listening to wallpaper. I am just as interested in poetry or whatever or art, and always have been, that's been my hang-up, you know—continually trying to be Shakespeare or whatever it is. That's what I'm doing, I'm not pissing about. I consider I'm up against *them.* I'm not competing myself against Elvis. Rock just happens to be the media which I was born into, it was the one, that's all. Those people picked up paint brushes, and Van Gogh probably wanted to be Renoir or whoever went before him just as I wanted to be Elvis or whatever the shit it is. I'm not interested in good guitarists. I'm in the game of all those things, of concept and philosophy, ways of life, and whole movements in history. Just like Van Gogh was or any other of those fuckin' people—they are no more or less than I am or Yoko is—they were just living in those days. I'm interested in expressing myself like they expressed it, in some way that will mean something to people in any country, in any language, and at any time in history.

When did you realize, that what you were doing transcended . . .

People like me are aware of their so-called genius at ten, eight, nine . . . I always wondered, 'why has nobody discovered me?' In school, didn't they see that I'm cleverer than anybody in this school? That the teachers are stupid, too? That all they had was information that I didn't need.

I got fuckin' lost in being at high school. I used to say to me auntie 'You throw my fuckin' poetry out, and you'll regret it when I'm famous,' and she threw the bastard stuff out.

Opposite: John and his Aunt

I never forgave her for not treating me like a fuckin' genius or whatever I was, when I was a child.

". . . tried to beat me into being Paul McCartney."

It was obvious to me. Why didn't they put me in art school? Why didn't they train me? Why would they keep forcing me to be a fuckin' cowboy like the rest of them? I was different, I was always different. Why didn't anybody notice me?

A couple of teachers would notice me, encourage me to be something or other, to draw or to paint—express myself. But most of the time they were trying to beat me into being a fuckin' dentist or a teacher. And then the fuckin' fans tried to beat me into being a fuckin' Beatle or an Engelbert Humperdinck, and the critics tried to beat me into being Paul McCartney.

YOKO: So you were very deprived in a way . . .

JOHN: That's what makes me what I am. It comes out, the people I meet have to say it themselves, because we get fuckin' kicked. Nobody says it, so you scream it: look at me, a genius, for fuck's sake! What do I have to do to prove to you son-of-a-bitches what I can do, and who I am? Don't dare, don't you dare fuckin' dare criticize my work like that. You, who don't know anything about it.

Fuckin' bullshit!

I know what Zappa is going through, and a half. I'm just coming out of it. I just have been in school again. I've had teachers ticking me off and marking my work. If nobody can recognize what I am then fuck 'em, it's the same for Yoko . . .

YOKO: That's why it's an amazing thing: after somebody has done something like the Beatles, they think that he's sort of satisfied, where actually the Beatles . . .

JOHN: The Beatles was nothing.

YOKO: It was like cutting him down to a smaller size than he is.

Yoko as important as Paul or Dylan

John: I learned lots from Paul and George, in many ways, but they learned a damned sight lot from me—they learned a fucking lot from me. It's like George Martin, or anybody: just come back in 20 years' time and see what we're doing, and see who's doing what—don't put me—don't sort of mark my papers like I'm top of the math class or did I come in Number One in English Language, because I never did. Just assess me on what I am and what comes out of me mouth, and what me work is, don't mark me in classrooms. It's like I've just left school again! I just graduated from the school of Show Biz or whatever it was called.

Who do you think is good today? In any arts . . .

The unfortunate thing about egomaniacs is that they don't take much attention of other people's work. I only assess people on whether they are a danger to me or my work or not.

Yoko is as important to me as Paul and Dylan rolled into one. I don't think she will get recognition until she's dead. There's me, and maybe I could count the people on one hand that have any conception of what she is or what her mind is like, or what her work means to this fuckin' idiotic generation. She has the hope that she might be recognized. If I can't get recognized, and I'm doing it in a fuckin' clown's costume, I'm doing it on the streets, you know, I don't know what—I admire Yoko's work.

I admire "Fluxus," a New York-based group of artists founded by George Macuinas. I really think what they do is beautiful and important.

I admire Andy Warhol's work, I admire Zappa a bit, but he's a fuckin' intellectual—I can't think of anybody else. I admire people from the past. I admire Fellini. A few that Yoko's educated me to . . . She's educated me into things that I didn't

Fellini, Zappa, Little Richard and Chuck Berry

know about before, because of the scene I was in; I'm getting to know some other great work that's been going on now and in the past—there is all sorts going on.

I still love Little Richard, and I love Jerry Lee Lewis. They're like primitive painters . . .

Chuck Berry is one of the all-time great poets, a rock poet you could call him. He was well advanced of his time lyric-wise. We all owe a lot to him, including Dylan. I've loved everything he's done, ever. He was in a different class from the other performers, he was in the tradition of the great blues artists but he really wrote his own stuff—I know Richard did, but Berry *really* wrote stuff, just the lyrics were fantastic, even though we didn't know what he was saying half the time.

YOKO: I'm really getting into it.

JOHN: We are both showing each other's experience to each other. When you play Yoko's music, I had the same thing: I had to open up to hear it—I had to get out the concept of what I wanted to hear . . . I had to allow abstract art or music in. She had to do the same for rock and roll, it was an intellectual exercise, because we're all boxed in. We are all in little boxes, and somebody has to go in and rip your fuckin' head open for you to allow something else in.

A drug will do it. Acid will box your head open. Some artists will do it, but they usually have to be dead two hundred years to do it. All I ever learned in art school was about Van Gogh and stuff; they didn't teach me anything about anybody that was alive now, or they never taught me about Marcel Duchamp which I despised them for. Yoko has taught me about Duchamp and what he did, which is just out of this world. He would just put a bike wheel on display and he would say this is art, you cunts. He wasn't

Opposite: Chuck Berry

Andy Warhol

Dali; Dali was all right, but he's like Mick, you know. I love Dali, but fuckin' Duchamp was spot on. He was the first one to do that, just take an object from the street and put his name on it, and say this is art because I say it is.

Why Warhol?

Because he is an original, and he's great. He is an original great and he is in so much pain. He's got his fame, he's got his own cinema and all of that. I don't dig that junkie fag scene he lives in; I don't know whether he lives like that or what. I dig Heinz Soup cans. That was something, that wasn't just a pop art, or some stupid art. Warhol said it, nobody's else has said it—Heinz Soup. He's said that to us, and I thanked him for it.

What do you think of Fellini?

Fellini's just like Dali, I suppose. It's a great meal to go and see Fellini, a great meal for your senses.

Like *Citizen Kane*, that's something else, too. Poor old Orson, he goes on Dick Cavett, and says 'Please love me, now I'm a big fat man, and I've eaten all this food, and I did so well when I was younger, I can act, I can direct, and you're all very kind to me, but at the moment I don't do anything.'

Do you see a time when you'll retire?

No. I couldn't, you know.

Yoko: He'll probably work until he's eighty or until he dies.

John: I can't foresee it. Even when you're a cripple you carry on painting. I would paint if I couldn't move. It doesn't matter, you see, when I was saying what Yoko did with "Greenfield Morning"—took half an inch she taped and none of us knew what we were doing, and I saw her create something. I saw her start from scratch

Opposite:
Andy Warhol

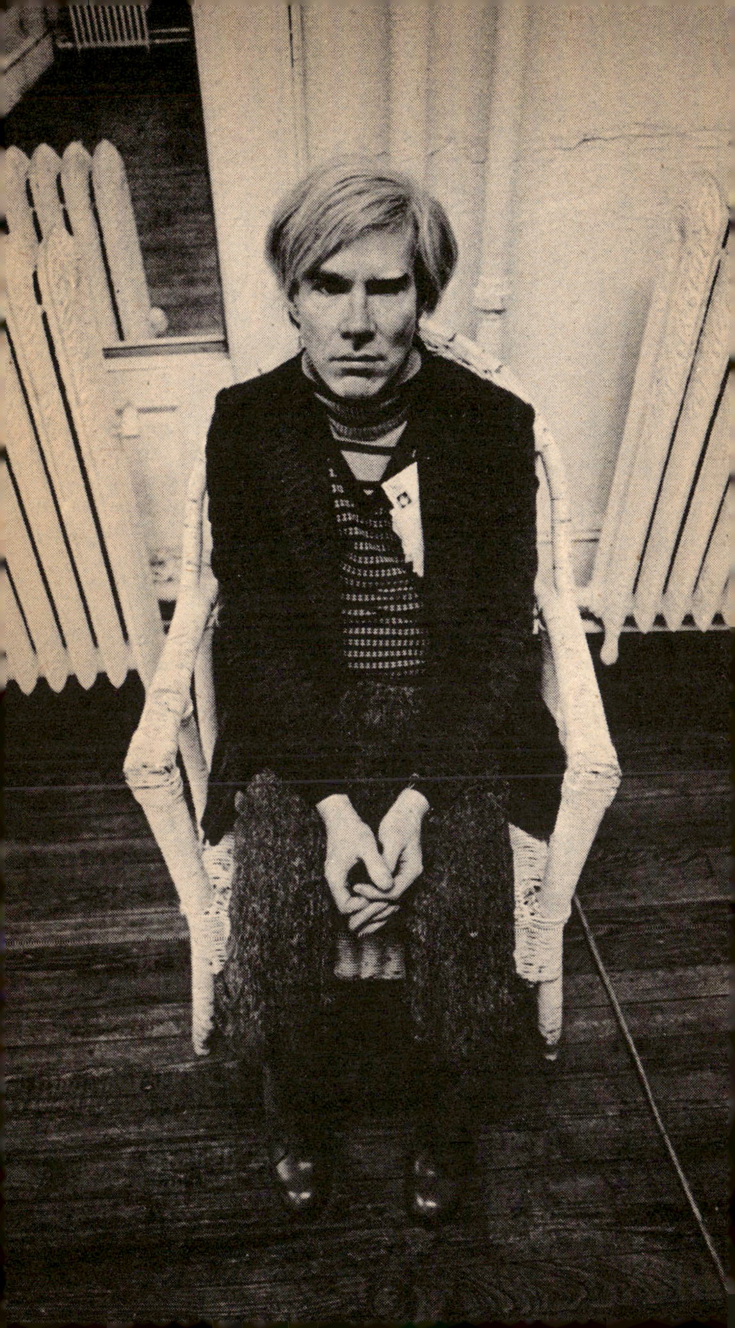

with something we would normally throw away. With the other stuff we did, we were all good in the backing and everything went according to plan, it was a good session, but with "Greenfield Morning" and "Paper Shoes" there was nothing there for her to work with. She just took nothing—the way Spector did—that's the way the genius shows through any media. You give Yoko or Spector a piece of tape, two inches of tape, they can create a symphony out of it. You don't have to be trained in rock and roll to be a singer; I didn't have to be trained to be a singer: I can sing. Singing is singing to people who enjoy what you're singing, not being able to hold notes—I don't have to be in rock and roll to create. When I'm an old man, we'll make wallpaper together, but just to have the same depth and impact. The message is the medium.

What is holding people back from understanding Yoko?

She was doing all right before she met Elvis. Howard Smith announced he was going to play her music on FM and all these idiots rang up and said 'Don't you dare play it, she split the Beatles.' She didn't split the Beatles and even if she did what does that have to do with it or her fucking record. She is a woman, and she's Japanese; there is racial prejudice against her and there is female prejudice against her. It's as simple as that.

Her work is far out, Yoko's bottom thing is as important as *Sgt. Pepper.* The real hip people know about it. There are a few people that know; there is a person in Paris who knows about her; a person in Moscow knows about her; there's a person in fucking China that knows about her. But in general, she can't be accepted, because she's too far out. It's hard to take. Her pain is such that she expresses herself in a way that hurts you—you cannot take it. That's why they couldn't take Van Gogh, it's too real, it hurts; that's why they kill you.

"I got the humour in her work"

How did you meet Yoko?

I'm sure I've told you this many times. How did I meet Yoko? There was a sort of underground clique in London; John Dunbar, who was married to Marianne Faithful, had an art gallery in London called Indica and I'd been going around to galleries a bit on my off days in between records. I'd been to see a Takis exhibition, I don't know if you know what that means, he does multiple electro-magnetic sculptures, and a few exhibitions in different galleries who showed these sort of unknown artists or underground artists. I got the word that this amazing woman was putting on a show next week and there was going to be something about people in bags, in black bags, and it was going to be a bit of a happening and all that. So I went down to a preview of the show. I got there the night before it opened. I went in—she didn't know who I was or anything—I was wandering around, there was a couple of artsy type students that had been helping lying around there in the gallery, and I was looking at it and I was astounded. There was an apple on sale there for 200 quid, I thought it was fantastic—I got the humor in her work immediately. I didn't have to sort of have much knowledge about avant-garde or underground art, but the humor got me straight away. There was a fresh apple on a stand—this was before Apple—and it was 200 quid to watch the apple decompose. But there was another piece which really decided me for-or-against the artist, a ladder which led to a painting which was hung on the ceiling. It looked like a black canvas with a chain with a spy glass hanging on the end of it. This was near the door when you went in. I climbed the ladder, you look through the spy-glass and in tiny little letters it says 'yes.'

So it was positive. I felt relieved. It's a great relief when you get up the ladder and you look through the spyglass and it doesn't say 'no' or 'fuck you' or something, it said 'yes.'

I was very impressed and John Dunbar sort of introduced us—neither of us knew who the hell we were, she didn't know who I was, she'd only heard of Ringo I think, it means apple in Japanese. And John Dunbar had been sort of hustling her saying 'that's a good patron, you must go and talk to him or do something' because I was looking for action, I was expecting a happening and things like that. John Dunbar insisted she say hello to the millionaire, you know what I mean. And she came up and handed me a card which said "Breathe" on it, one of her instructions, so I just went (pant). This was our meeting.

Then I went away and the second time I met her at a gallery opening of Claes Oldenberg in London. We were very shy, we sort of nodded at each other and we didn't know—she was standing behind me, I sort of looked away because I'm very shy with people, especially chicks. We just sort of smiled and stood frozen together in this cocktail party thing.

The next thing was she came to me to get some backing—like all the bastard underground do—for a show she was doing. She gave me her Grapefruit book and I used to read it and sometimes I'd get very annoyed by it; it would say things like "paint until you drop dead" or "bleed" and then sometimes I'd be very enlightened by it and I went through all the changes that people go through with her work—sometimes I'd have it

In love

by the bed and I'd open it and it would say something nice and it would be alright and then it would say something heavy and I wouldn't like it. There was all that and then she came to me to get some backing for a show and it was half a wind show. I gave her the money to back it and the show was—this was in a place called Lisson Gallery, another one of those underground places. For this whole show everything was in half: there was half a bed, half a room, half of everything, all beautifully cut in half and all painted white. And I said to her 'why don't you sell the other half in bottles?' having caught on by then what the game was and she did that—this is still before we'd had any nuptials—and we still have the bottles from the show, it's my first. It was presented as "Yoko Plus Me"—that was our first public appearance. I didn't even go to see the show, I was too uptight.

When did you realize that you were in love with her?

It was beginning to happen; I would start looking at her book and that but I wasn't quite aware what was happening to me and then she did a thing called Dance Event where different cards kept coming through the door every day saying "Breathe" and "Dance" and "Watch all the lights until dawn," and they upset me or made me happy depending on how I felt.

I'd get very upset about it being intellectual or all fucking avant-garde, then I'd like it and then I wouldn't. Then I went to India with the Maharoonie and we were corresponding. The letters were still formal but they just had a little side to them. I nearly took her to India as I said but I still wasn't sure for what reason, I was still sort of kidding myself, with sort of artistic reasons, and all that.

When we got back from India we were talking

to each other on the phone. I called her over, it was the middle of the night and Cyn was away, and I thought well now's the time if I'm gonna get to know her anymore. She came to the house and I didn't know what to do; so we went upstairs to my studio and I played her all the tapes that I'd made, all this far out stuff, some comedy stuff, and some electronic music. She was suitably impressed and then she said well let's make one ourselves so we made "Two Virgins." It was midnight when we started "Two Virgins," it was dawn when we finished, and then we made love at dawn. It was very beautiful.

What was it like getting married? Did you enjoy it?

It was very romantic. It's all in the song, "The Ballad of John and Yoko," if you want to know how it happened, it's in there. Gibraltar was like a little sunny dream. I couldn't find a white suit—I had sort of off-white corduroy trousers and a white jacket. Yoko had all white on.

What was your first peace event?

The first peace event was the Amsterdam Bed Peace when we got married.

What was that like—that was your first re-exposure to the public.

It was a nice high. We were on the seventh floor of the Hilton looking over Amsterdam—it was very crazy, the press came expecting to see us fucking in bed—they all heard John and Yoko were going to fuck in front of the press for peace. So when they all walked in—about 50 or 60 reporters flew over from London all sort of very edgy, and we were just sitting in pajamas saying "Peace, Brother" and that was it. On the peace thing there's lots of heavy discussions with intellectuals about how you should do it and how you shouldn't.

The Bed-In and Golda Meir

When you got alone, did you feel satisfied with the Bed Peace . . . ?

They were great events when you think that the world newspaper headlines were the fact that we were a married couple in bed talking about peace. It was one of our greater episodes. It was like being on tour without moving, sort of a big promotional thing. I think we did a good job for what we were doing, which was trying to get people to own up.

You chose the word "peace" and not "love," or another word that means the same thing. What did you like about the word "peace"?

Yoko and I were discussing our different lives and careers when we first got together. What we had in common in a way, was that she'd done things for peace like standing in Trafalgar Square in a black bag and things like that—we were just trying to work out what we could do—and the Beatles had been singing about "love" and things. So we pooled our resources and came out with the Bed Peace—it was some way of doing something together that wouldn't involve me standing in Trafalgar Square in a black bag because I was too nervous to do that. Yoko didn't want to do anything that wasn't for peace.

Did you ever get any reaction from political leaders?

I don't know about the Bed-In. We got reaction to sending acorns—different heads of state actually planted their acorns, lots of them wrote to us answering about the acorns. We sent acorns to practically everybody in the world.

Who answered?

Well, I believe Golda Meir said 'I don't know who they are but if it's for peace, we're for it' or something like that. Scandinavia, somebody or other planted it. I think Haile Selassie planted his, I'm not sure. Some Queen somewhere. There was quite a few people that understood the idea.

Prime Minister Trudeau

Did you send one to Queen Elizabeth?

We sent one to Harold Wilson, I don't think we got a reply from Harold, did we?

What was it like meeting [Canadian] Prime Minister Trudeau? What was his response to you?

He was interested in us because he thought we might represent some sort of youth faction—he wants to know, like everybody does, really. I think he was very nervous—he was more nervous than we were when we met. We talked about everything—just anything you can think of. We spent about 40 minutes—it was 5 minutes longer than he'd spent with heads of state which was the great glory of the time. He'd read *In His Own Write*, my book, and things like that. He liked the poetry side of it. We just wanted to see what they did, how they worked.

You appeared in the bags for Hanratty.

For Hanratty, yes, we did a sort of bag event, but it wasn't us in the bag it was somebody else. The best thing we did in a bag together was a press conference in Vienna. When they were showing Yoko's *Rape* on Austrian TV—they commissioned us to make the film and then we went over to Vienna to see it.

It was like a hotel press conference. We kept them out of the room. We came down the elevator in the bag and we went in and we got comfortable and they were all ushered in. It was a very strange scene because they'd never seen us before, or heard—Vienna is a pretty square place. A few people were saying, 'C'mon, get out of the bags.' And we wouldn't let 'em see us. They all stood back saying 'Is it really John and Yoko?' and 'What are you wearing and why are you doing this?' We said, 'This is total communications with no prejudice.' It was just great.

The erotic lithographs

They asked us to sing and we sang a few numbers. Yoko was singing a Japanese folk song, very nicely, just very straight we did it. And they never did see us.

What kind of response did you get to the 'War Is Over' poster?

We got a big response. The people that got in touch with us understood what a grand event it was apart from the message itself. We got just thank you's from lots of youths around the world—for all the things we were doing—that inspired *them* to do something. We had a lot of response from other than pop fans, which was interesting, from all walks of life and age. If I walk down the street now I'm more liable to get talked to about peace than anything I've done. The first thing that happened in New York was just walking down the street and a woman just came to me and said 'Good luck with the peace thing,' that's what goes on mainly—it's not about "I Want to Hold Your Hand." And that was interesting—it bridged a lot of gaps.

What do you think of those erotic lithographs now?

I don't think about them.

Why did you do them?

Because somebody said do some lithographs and I was in a drawing mood and I drew them.

You also did a scene for the Tynan play. How did that come about?

I met Tynan a few times around and about and he just said—this is about two years ago or more—he just said I'm getting all these different people to write something erotic, will you do it? And I told him that if I come up with something I'd do it and if I don't, I don't. So I came up with two lines, two or three lines which was the masturbation scene. It was a great childhood thing, everybody's been masturbating and trying

Opposite: *Two Virgins*

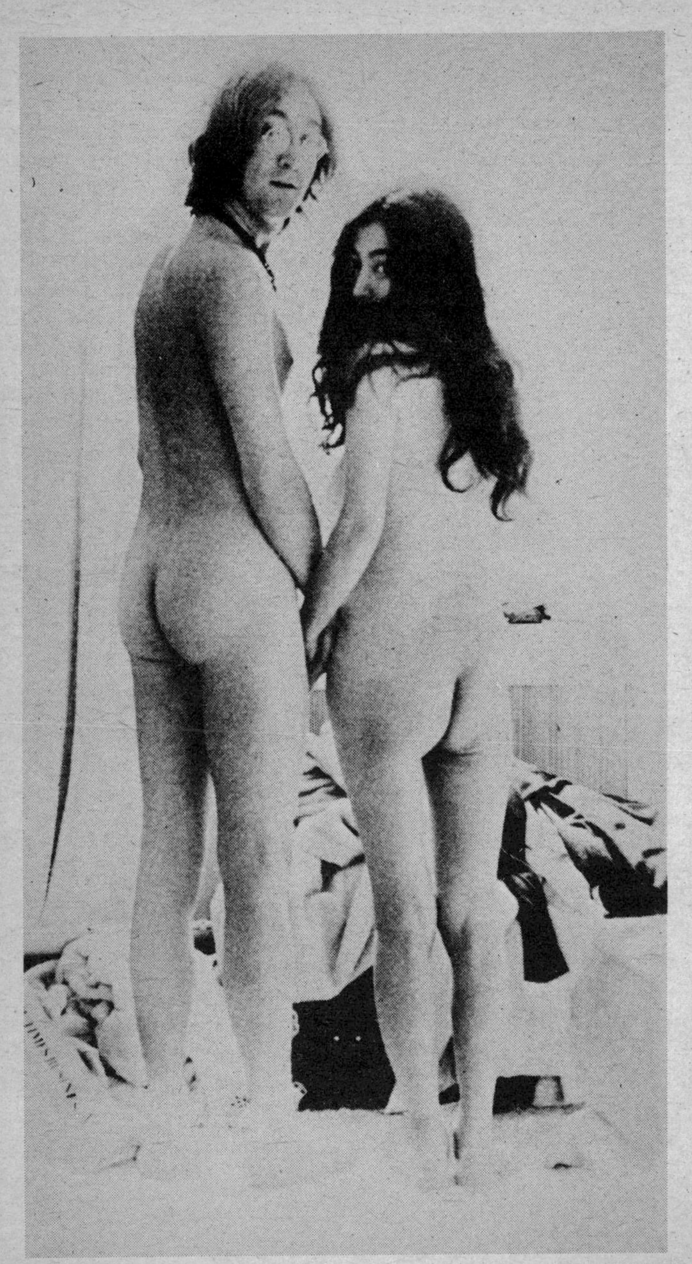

to think of something sexy and somebody'd shout Winston Churchill in the middle of it and break down. So I just wrote that down on a paper and told them to put whichever names in that suited the hero and they did it. I've never seen it.

What accounts for your great popularity?

Because I fuckin' did it. I copped out in that Beatle thing. I was like an artist that went off . . . Have you never heard of like Dylan Thomas and all them who never fuckin' wrote but just went up drinking and Brendan Behan and all of them, they died of drink . . . everybody that's done anything is like that. I just got meself in a party, I was an emperor, I had millions of chicks, drugs, drink, power and everybody saying how great I was. How could I get out of it? It was just like being in a fuckin' train. I couldn't get out.

I couldn't create, either. I created a little, it came out, but I was in the party and you don't get out of a thing like that. It was fantastic! I came out of the sticks, I didn't hear about anything—Van Gogh was the most far out thing I had ever heard of. Even London was something we used to dream of, and London's nothing. I came out of the fuckin' sticks to take over the world it seemed to me. I was enjoying it, and I was trapped in it, too. I couldn't do anything about it, I was just going along for the ride. I was hooked, just like a junkie.

What did being from Liverpool have to do with your art?

It was a port. That means it was less hick than somewhere in the English Midlands, like the American Midwest or whatever you call it. We were a port, the second biggest port in England, between Manchester and Liverpool. The North is where the money was made in the 1800s, that

was where all the brass and the heavy people were, and that's where the despised people were.

We were the ones that were looked down upon as animals by the Southerners, the Londoners. The Northerners in the States think that people are pigs down South and the people in New York think West Coast is hick. So we were hicksville.

We were a great amount of Irish descent and blacks and Chinamen, all sorts there. It was like San Francisco, you know. That San Francisco is something else! Why do you think Haight-Ashbury and all that happened there? It didn't happen in Los Angeles, it happened in San Francisco, where people are going. LA you pass through and get a hamburger.

There was nothing big in Liverpool; it wasn't American. It was going poor, a very poor city, and tough. But people have a sense of humor because they are in so much pain, so they are always cracking jokes. They are very witty, and it's an Irish place. It is where the Irish came when they ran out of potatoes, and it's where black people were left or worked as slaves or whatever.

It is cosmopolitan, and it's where the sailors would come home with the blues records from America on the ships. There is the biggest country and western following in England in Liverpool, besides London—always besides London, because there is more of it there.

I heard country and western music in Liverpool before I heard rock and roll. The people there—the Irish in Ireland are the same—they take their country and western music very seriously. There's a big heavy following of it. There were established folk, blues and country and western clubs in Liverpool before rock and roll and we were like the new kids coming out.

I remember the first guitar I ever saw. It belonged to a guy in a cowboy suit in a province of Liverpool, with stars, and a cowboy hat and a big dobro. They were real cowboys, and they took it seriously. There had been cowboys long before there was rock and roll.

What do you think of America?

What do you think of America?

I love it, and I hate it. America is where it's at. I should have been born in New York, I should have been born in the Village, that's where I belong. Why wasn't I born there? Paris was it in the 18th Century, London I don't think has ever been it except literary-wise when Wilde and Shaw and all of them were there. New York was it.

I regret profoundly that I was not an American and not born in Greenwich Village. That's where I should have been. It never works that way. Everybody heads toward the center, that's why I'm here now. I'm here just to breathe it. It might be dying and there might be a lot of dirt in the air that you breathe, but this is where it's happening. You go to Europe to rest, like in the country. It's so overpowering, America, and I'm such a fuckin' cripple, that I can't take much of it, it's too much for me.

YOKO: He's very New York, you know.

JOHN: I'm frightened of it. People are so aggressive, I can't take all that I need to go home, I need to have a look at the grass. I'm always writing about my English garden. I need the trees and the grass; I need to go into the country, because I can't stand too much people.

Right after Sergeant Pepper *George came to San Francisco.*

George went over in the end. I was all for going and living in the Haight. In my head, I thought, 'Acid is it, and let's go, I'll go there.' I was going to go there, but I'm too nervous to do anything, actually. I thought I'll go there and we'll live there and I'll make music and live like that. Of course, it didn't come true.

But it happened in San Francisco. It happened all right, didn't it. I mean it goes down in history. I love it. It's like when Shaw was in England, and they all went to Paris; and I see all that in New York, San Francisco and London, even London. We created something there—Mick and us, we didn't know what we were doing, but we were all talking, blabbing over coffee, like they must have done in Paris, talking about paintings . . . Me, Burdon and Brian Jones would be up night and day talking about music, playing records, and blabbing and arguing and getting drunk. It's beautiful history, and it happened in all these different places. I just miss New York. In New York they have their own cool clique. Yoko came out of that.

This is the first time I'm really seeing it, because I was always too nervous, I was always the famous Beatle. Dylan showed it to me once on sort of a guided tour around the Village, but I never got any feel of it. I just knew Dylan was New York, and I always sort of wished I'd been there for the experience that Bob got from living around here.

What is the nature of your relationship with Bob?

It's sort of an acquaintance, because we were so nervous whenever we used to meet. It was always under the most nervewracking circumstances, and I know I was always uptight and I know Bobby was. We were together and we spent some time, but I would always be too paranoid or I would be aggressive or vice versa and we didn't really speak. But we spent a lot of time together.

He came to me house, which was Kenwood,

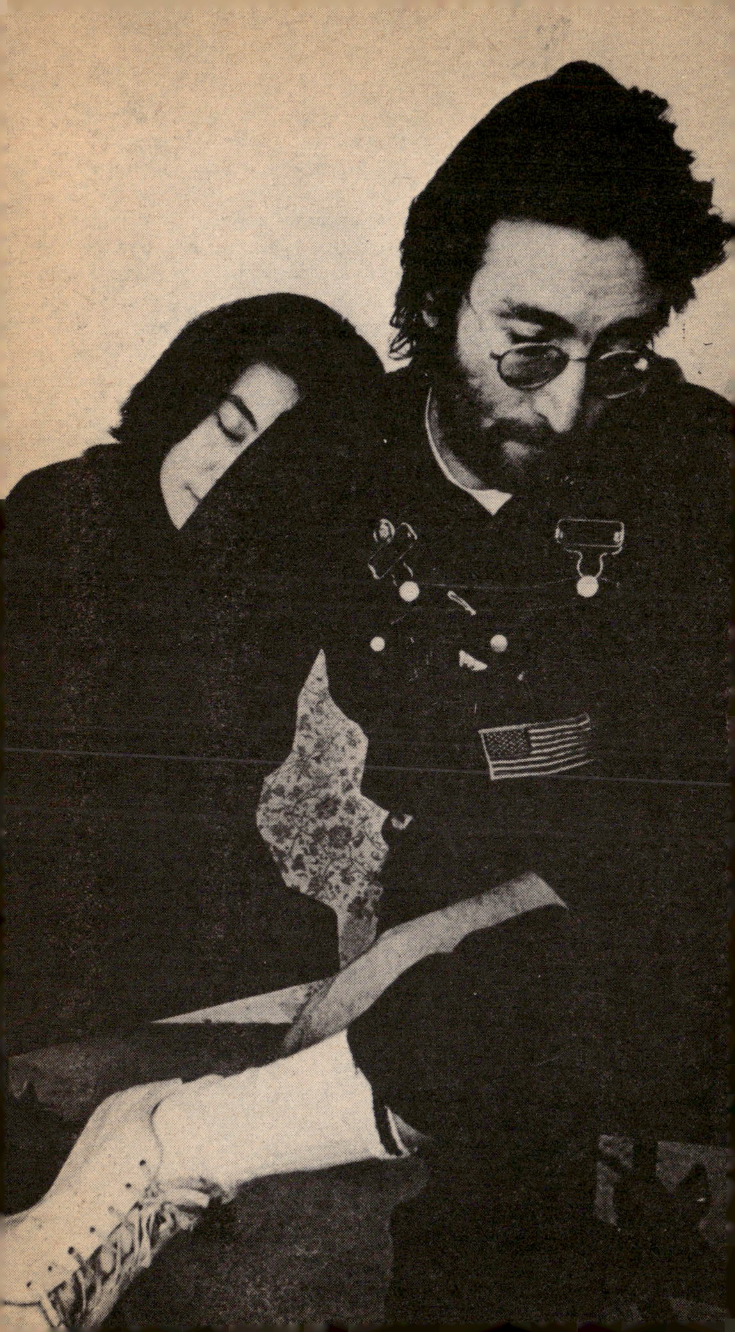

Relations with Bob Dylan

can you imagine it, and I didn't know where to put him in this sort of bourgeois home life I was living; I didn't know what to do and things like that. I used to go to his hotel rather, and I loved him, you know, because he wrote some beautiful stuff. I used to love that, his so-called protest things. I listen to his words, he used to come with his acetate and say 'Listen to this, John, and did you hear the words?' I said that doesn't matter, the sound is what counts—the overall thing. I had too many father figures and I liked words, too, so I liked a lot of the stuff he did. You don't have to hear what Bob Dylan's saying, you just have to hear the way he says it.

Do you see him as a great?

No, I see him as another poet, or as competition. You read my books that were written before I heard of Dylan or read Dylan or anybody, it's the same. I didn't come after Elvis and Dylan, I've been around always. But if I see or meet a great artist, I love 'em. I go fanatical about them for a short period, and then I get over it. If they wear green socks I'm liable to wear green socks for a period too.

When was the last time you saw Bob?

He came to our house with George after the Isle of Wight and when I had written "Cold Turkey".

Yoko: And his wife.

John: I was just trying to get him to record. We had just put him on piano for "Cold Turkey" to make a rough tape but his wife was pregnant or something and they left. He's calmed down a lot now.

I just remember before that we were both in shades and both on fucking junk, and all these freaks around us and Ginsberg and all those people. I was anxious as shit.

You were in that movie with him, that hasn't been released?

Rough picture of immediate future

I've never seen it but I'd love to see it. I was always so paranoid and Bob said 'I want you to be in this film.' He just wanted to me to be in the film.

I thought why? What? He's going to put me down; I went all through this terrible thing.

In the film, I'm just blabbing off and commenting all the time, like you do when you're very high or stoned. I had been up all night. We were being smart alecks, it's terrible. But it was his scene, that was the problem for me. It was his movie. I was on his territory, that's why I was so nervous. I was on his session.

You're going back to London. What's a rough picture of your immediate future, say the next three months.

I'd like to just vanish just a bit. It wore me out, New York. I love it. I'm just sort of fascinated by it, like a fucking monster. Doing the films was a nice way of meeting a lot of people. I think we've both said and done enough for a few months, especially with this article. I'd like to get out of the way and wait till they all . . .

Do you have a rough picture of the next few years?

Oh no, I couldn't think of the next few years; it's abysmal thinking of how many years there are to go, millions of them. I just play it by the week. I don't think much ahead of a week.

I have no more to ask.

Well, fancy that.

Do you have anything to add?

No, I can't think of anything positive and heart-warming to win your readers over.

Do you have a picture of "when I'm 64"?

No, no. I hope we're a nice old couple living off the coast of Ireland or something like that—looking at our scrapbook of madness.

PHOTOGRAPHS:

Pages 5, 13, 47, 161, and 165, by courtesy of
16 Magazine; 68, 95, 117, 127 (top), and 143 Ethan Russell;
15, 28 and 89, Rex Features; 17, Michael T. Putland;
23, 125, 141, 153, 171, 177, and 187, Annie Leibovitz;
35, Lynn Adler; 57, Shep Sherbell;
81, Scheler/Black Star; 102, Bob Gruen; 50 and 107, Joseph Sia;
111, Barry Davies; 65, 135, and 177, Pix Inc.;
127 (bottom), Alan Howard; 133, UPI; 137, Stephen Goldblatt;
147, Eric Hayes; 157, Jeff Mayer; 159, Ed Caraeff;
169, Henry Diltz; 181, John and Yoko.